RUGBY
TACTICS

Peter Winder

A & C Black · London

First published 1991 by
A & C Black (Publishers) Ltd
35 Bedford Row, London WC1R 4JH

© 1991 Peter Winder

ISBN 0 7136 3449 9

A CIP catalogue record for this book is available
from the British Library.

Printed and bound in Great Britain by
Courier International Ltd,
East Kilbride, Scotland

Contents

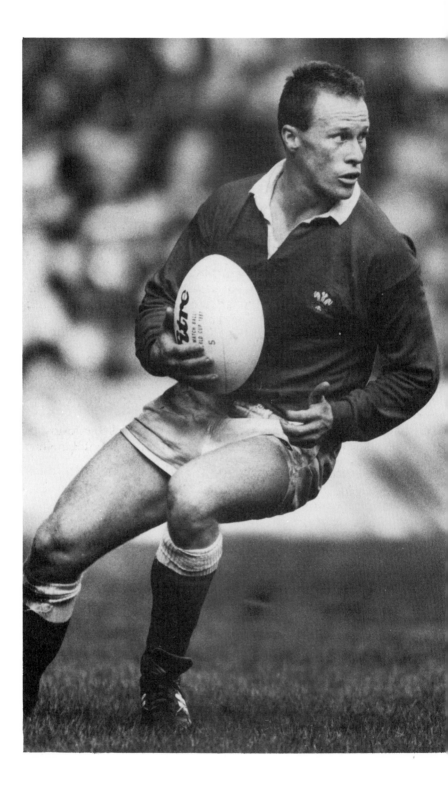

Introduction

Rugby football is a competitive, physical-contact game that requires tremendous commitment and enthusiasm for successful participation. It is exhilarating and exciting for both player and spectator, providing enjoyment for all concerned. Rugby also provides a suitable outlet for the controlled release of any frustration or aggression within the structured framework of an athletically demanding sport.

Players enjoy themselves more when their performance is appreciated, with their efforts positively contributing to the specific achievements of their playing unit and overall success of the team.

To be able to fulfil his potential, every player needs to have:

1 mastered the basic techniques and skills necessary to participate successfully in rugby football
2 a good understanding of the individual playing requirements of his position
3 an awareness of his expected contribution to and role in the performance of his playing unit and its function in attempting to improve the team effort
4 a knowledge of the principles of play, unit and team strategies
5 a thorough knowledge of the laws of the game, and
6 tactical awareness and understanding.

Rugby football is continually changing and developing with coaches and players introducing new ideas and tactical initiatives to improve team performances and help to achieve successful results. Every coach must be aware of his responsibility to help players to develop and improve their technical performances, and tactical awareness and application. This book has been written as a guide for coaches and players, to highlight the many different features of rugby football and stimulate greater thought about the purpose and tactics of the game.

Note. Throughout the book coaches and players are referred to individually as 'he'. This should of course be taken to mean 'he or she'.

(Left) *After safely catching the high ball, Paul Thorburn (Wales) assesses the options and prepares to perform the most appropriate action to exploit possession*

1 The importance and relevance of tactics

Tactical awareness and understanding must concern every player, and he also requires a good knowledge and practical appreciation of the laws of the game. Teams should be organised by their coach to deal with every situation that they will encounter during a match, including all restarts, set pieces phases of transitional play, kicking for position and penalty moves. Players must be made aware of their individual and collective responsibilities for each phase of play. The coach must work in conjunction with the players to achieve cohesion within the independent units of the forwards and threequarters, ensuring that they are linked together successfully by the half-backs to function effectively as a team.

The individual playing position determines the particular techniques and skills that each player needs to successfully participate in a match. The required levels of tactical understanding, application and sophistication depend on his involvement in making key decisions during play. However all players must be familiar with the agreed basic pattern of play and made aware of the tactical team approach in all situations, knowing what they are expected to contribute and achieve during their involvement in competitive games.

Tactics are the means of achieving a successful performance during all phases of play, skilfully executing certain procedures and ploys in an attempt to win the match. The emphasis is on securing possession from every competitive situation, then dominating the opposition by driving forwards and moving the ball around the field, advancing over the gain line towards and across the opponents' goal line to score points and thereby win the game. Players constantly attempt to exploit space and create scoring possibilities for themselves or team-mates, while denying their opponents the same opportunities. It is the manner in which the players attempt to achieve this objective from each playing situation and field position that constitutes tactical application, endeavour and enterprise.

The methods of securing possession and the cohesion of the individual players into successful units, to function effectively and purposefully under the limitations of the laws of the game are the tactical considerations. Rugby football involves individual players competing directly against one another for supremacy of achievement in their performance. The manner and methods in which players attempt to outmanoeuvre, pressurise and dominate their opponents are determined by their individual abilities and

The individual and collective abilities of the forwards to secure regularly quality possession at the line-outs affect tactical selection and execution

skills, applied in conjunction with the team strategy. The basic pattern of play provides an agreed structure that gives purpose, coherence and rhythm to particular unit and overall team play.

A team should always be prepared to play to their individual and unit strengths, attempting to gain control of the match by dominating their opponents and outwitting them, preventing them from determining or controlling the pattern of play. Once a team become familiar with their opponents' intentions and alter their deployment of players and defensive strategies to restrict and counter their effectiveness, players should be able to adapt and extend their pattern of play to exploit the new areas of weakness resulting from these developments. It is important that a team grasp the initiative from their opponents and maintain it by being unpredictable, constantly altering the speed of their preparation time for set pieces, regularly changing the direction of attack, and trying to disrupt their opponents from settling into a comfortable routine and rhythm.

By creating many different situations during training, players can develop greater confidence in their abilities and learn to quickly assess all the available options, selecting the most suitable and performing the most appropriate action for their team's benefit. Great attacking opportunities can be created when a team receive possession of the ball as a result of a poor clearance kick from the other team. Developing the players' confidence and expertise to exploit these opportunities is one of the most important roles of the coach. Acquiring the basic techniques of catching, running and passing are obviously important requirements for every player, but it is the manner in which these skills are executed in the game situation that determines the success of the performance.

The significance of coaching

The significance of coaching in improving tactical appreciation and understanding has been aptly demonstrated by the successful and improved achievements of touring teams. During visits to different countries, coaches have often needed to adapt the playing style and technical application of their teams to cope with the different conditions and interpretations of the laws of the game. It is often necessary to revise existing strategies and devise new ones to comply with the discrepancies, without adversely affecting the effectiveness of the team effort.

All successful teams have a good, pragmatic coach organising their sessions, guiding practices to improve individual, unit and overall team performances. To adopt the best tactical approach the coach must select and devise strategies that complement the players' abilities, as well as compensate for any physical or technical weaknesses, to achieve and maximise opportunities to win the ball and use possession effectively.

Coaches need to earn the players' respect and confidence by demonstrating a thorough knowledge and depth of understanding of the basics and intricacies of rugby football. Once this has been achieved and the coach has earned the players' trust, different tactical ploys and unique ideas can be practised, refined and perfected for inclusion in the repertoire of moves in the overall game plan.

It is important for the coach and players to identify particular recurring situations that provide:

1 a consistently good supply of possession to create potential scoring opportunities
2 potential attacking opportunities for the other team.

Once these diverse situations have been acknowledged, it is necessary to devise and implement suitable and effective strategies that can exploit, successfully defend against and counter eventualities.

Tactics consist of a careful creation, selection and application of relevant strategic ploys to ensure that players achieve the maximum success for their collective efforts in every situation. The coach and players need to identify the playing situations that they can continually exploit to their advantage by rehearsing suitable tactical ploys that prove effective on a regular basis. The emphasis in attack and defence should be on applying and maintaining pressure on the opposing players as a result of purposefully co-ordinated actions.

Coaches must prepare players to correctly assess developing situations and be capable of altering the team strategy to exploit the weaknesses and counter the obvious strengths and advantages of their opponents. For example, in a team in which the forwards are physically relatively small and limited in stature, the unit should prepare carefully for the scrummages and delay entering into direct competition with their opponents until the scrum-half is in possession and ready to deliver the ball. The hooker should also be in a comfortable striking position before the front rows meet. As soon as the scrummage is formed the hooker should signal to the scrum-half to feed the ball as quickly as possible, reducing the duration of this influential forward encounter. This will limit the opportunities for the opposition to take advantage of their physical prowess and dominate the scrummage.

Management and communication

Skilful play results from sound coaching and development of techniques necessary to play the game. Effective tactical application can also result from good coaching, careful planning, sound preparation and team discipline. The coach, team manager and captain should involve all the players in tactical discussions, providing them with the opportunity to express their ideas and opinions by holding regular forums before and sometimes during training, as well as during post-match analysis of competitive performances. The management team must also be aware of the pattern of play and hold confidential meetings to agree upon the selection of the most suitable and competent players. Good coaching and management skills, involving regular liaison with the captain, as well as open and honest discussion with the other players, result in an agreed game plan or system of play suitable to capitalise on the strengths of the players.

Good club organisation and administration succeed in keeping current players informed of developments and help to attract new players, having a positive influence on recruitment. Players are attracted to different clubs because of their playing style, achievements and reputation, sensibly joining a club that plays a type of game suitable for them to display their particular individual strengths.

Systems of play

There are many debates and discussions that compare and contrast the benefits of one system of play with another. Direct comparisons are made between teams that play a power game, capitalising on their forward strengths to dominate opponents, and teams that play an expansive game that utilises the elusive-running and handling skills of their players. These are the two basic systems of play and coaching philosophies that exist in rugby football.

Although a popular discussion topic at social gatherings, this direct comparison of the playing systems is a very limited and outdated view of tactical selection, application and endeavour. The growth in leisure time, increased popularity of the game, the involvement of television and the influence of commercial interests in rugby football have resulted in the introduction of competitive league tables with promotion and relegation, as well as the inauguration of the World Cup. All these developments have increased the pressures on all players involved in the sport, particularly increasing the demands of club and representative rugby, necessitating an improvement in the levels of players' commitment and dedication. This has produced a marked improvement in the standards of physical fitness, conditioning, technical expertise and consequently the speed at which the game is played.

As a result, more time is being allocated to the preparation of teams for competitive matches at all levels, with coaches and players adopting a more dedicated approach. This has resulted in the development of greater levels of understanding and familiarity between players than before, improving their standards of performance and confidence in one another. Consequently players are prepared to experiment and attempt different ploys during practice sessions, which has proved a positive influence on the development of team strategies. There have been many developments of more sophisticated tactical enterprise in recent years: for example, the driving maul, with players securing possession and concentrating their forward momentum through the centre of the maul, as well as rolling and driving around the fringes.

It is the attention of the coach and players to the intricate details of securing and using possession that makes rugby football such an entertaining, interesting and enjoyable spectacle. The numerous tactical considerations include the different approaches and contributions of individual and unit players to function effectively and efficiently throughout their involvement in the game. These include:

1 individual players' roles in attempting to secure possession of the ball during the starts and restarts of the game: taking and receiving kick-offs and drop-outs

2 ploys at the set pieces of line-outs and scrummages to secure possession and disrupt the efforts of the other team, preventing them from winning, securing and utilising the ball

3 deciding when it is appropriate to ruck and when to maul the ball, providing the forwards are equally proficient in performing and executing both techniques successfully

4 interpassing between the scrum-half and back-row forwards to commit opponents, continuing the forward momentum to cross the gain line

5 selecting and successfully executing a repertoire of passing movements between the threequarters, making good and effective use of hard-earned possession, attempting to improve territorial position and create scoring opportunities

6 the appropriate selection and execution of penalty ploys and moves

7 deciding when to kick the ball for touch to pressurise opponents or to improve the field position

8 defensive ploys of the forwards and threequarters at the set pieces and during the transitional phases of play

9 selecting and executing the most appropriate technique or action in a given situation for the team's benefit.

There are many factors that can affect the selection of one tactical ploy in preference to others, contributing to the framework of the team strategy. It is vitally important that a team's tactical approach is the most appropriate to encompass the skills and talents of all the players. The coach must assess the players' capabilities, selecting the most relevant strategy and developing a suitable tactical approach for each situation that the team is likely to confront during their participation in a game.

The preparation must ensure that the players are familiar with their roles within the team and capable of making an important, purposeful and successful contribution. The coach must instil team discipline through sound organisation that results in a co-ordinated and co-operative effort from the players, complementing the efforts of each other.

For example, when the ball is kicked in an attempt to improve territorial position and produce good attacking positions to exploit, or to relieve the pressure imposed by their opponents, supporting and covering the kicks involves a tremendous amount of running for the chasing support players.

Therefore any players making the decision to kick the ball during play must communicate that intention to team-mates as quickly as possible. By devising a code of signals, the players should be able to communicate the direction and distance that the ball is intended to travel. Providing the execution of the kick is accurate, a team can reduce the amount of running involved by sharing the work, delegating different roles and responsibilities to individual players or units. Most teams have a strategy for following up and covering the remainder of the field when they have decided to take a penalty kick at goal; it would be sensible to include a similar strategy during open play, when the ball is kicked upfield.

Tactical changes

The coach's most difficult task is to convince players of the benefit of adopting a particular system and style of play, thereby attempting to develop a successful team strategy. Some players are reluctant to adapt or change their playing style, particularly when their efforts have proved successful in the past. This concern is understandable and requires the coach to adopt a sympathetic approach when attempting to incorporate changes in the manner that players apply themselves and perform in different situations.

To convince players of the value of adopting particular tactical changes to the team approach and altering the system of play to include different strategic ploys requires the coach to present a convincing and reasoned explanation of the need to implement the changes, demonstrating the benefits that will result from the modifications. Players cannot be expected to abandon methods and strategies that they have considered successful, however limited, without adequate justification and some evidence that the changes will enhance the team performance. On occasions, some developments are enforced as a result of changes in the laws of the game, making tactical modifications and refinements necessary in attempting to fulfil the demands, as well as endeavouring to exploit and take advantage of the imposed reforms for the team's benefit.

Both the coaching staff and players need to develop an open-minded approach and always be prepared to attempt the unpredictable when the opportunity presents itself. Every player must have confidence in his own ability as well as that of his team-mates and must be encouraged when attempting the unusual, unexpected and unorthodox. Conventional tactics are easily defeated through sound preparation, organisation and practice, it is the extraordinary, innovative and adventurous that proves effective and successful. Before players are encouraged to incorporate the unpredictable, they should rehearse and master its execution in training.

Players should always be capable of explaining the reasons for every action contained in their performance during a game. A good coach requests his players to justify certain decisions during training, searching for the motivation behind the execution of particular ploys and finding out what other options the player considered before selecting that particular one. Through careful and considerate questioning, the coach can determine whether the player correctly assessed the situation or simply reacted without thinking.

There are many situations during competitive fixtures when players execute a certain skill because they are under pressure or feel uncomfortable in possession of the ball. The pressure could be a result of the close proximity of the opposing players, receiving the ball in an unfamiliar field position, or fatigue. In these circumstances many players elect to kick the ball to relieve the pressure without considering any other worthwhile options.

The gain line and the tackle line

These are terms used by coaches to describe imaginary lines and explain the simple playing principle of going forwards whether a team are attacking with the ball or defending. The effectiveness of players' efforts can be clearly defined when explained in terms of crossing the gain line. Considerable

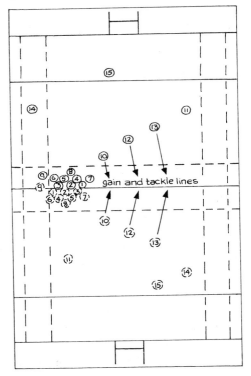

The threequarter formations create equal gain and tackle lines

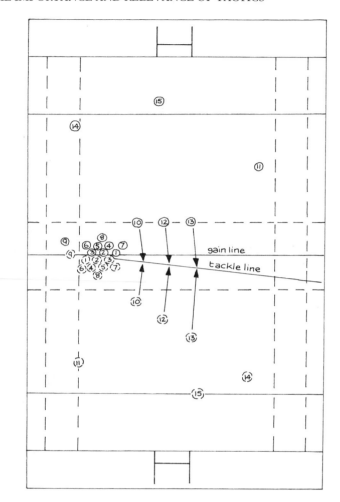

Defending threequarters are positioned in a line behind the feet of the number eight, increasing the pressure on the team receiving possession to make the tackle line superior to the gain line

reference is made during this book to the importance of the team in possession crossing the gain line, sometimes also referred to as the advantage line. The gain line passes through the centre of the source of possession, that is scrummages, line-outs, rucks and mauls, running parallel to the goal line.

The tackle line denotes the contact point where the players meet when the ball leaves the source of possession. The main objective and immediate intention of every defending player should be to limit his opponents' success and prevent the ball carrier from crossing the gain line. The aim of every attacking player is to move forwards, elude the defending players and advance beyond the gain line.

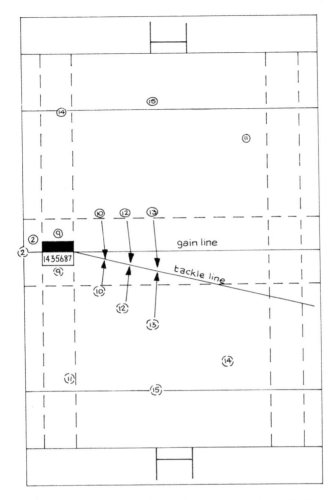

At the line-out the team not responsible for the throw-in are standing only 10 metres away in a straight-line formation, to pressurise the attacking team to make the tackle line superior to the gain line

The significance of physical fitness

The physical fitness, mental toughness, confidence and sound preparation of players determine their efforts on the playing field during a match situation. The players' levels of physical fitness and their abilities to anticipate developments during play also determine the selection of the methods adopted to secure possession of the ball, to maintain the forward momentum and resulting pressure on their opponents. All players must be fit enough to maintain their physical application, as well as their mental concentration, for the whole of the game. This can be achieved through active participation in structured physical conditioning and game-related practices organised by the coach.

The fitness levels and the range of the individual abilities of players are probably the most important factors that affect the selection of a suitable tactical game plan. Although the degree of success in performing certain technical features of the game is important, the effect of these on the team performance can be reduced by shrewd tactical selection and enterprise. For example, a niggling injury to one of the specialist line-out jumpers during the game could briefly have an adverse affect on this player's application and contribution during the set pieces of scrummages and line-outs. To limit the effects of this temporary injury problem, a team can alter their tactics during their throw-in at the line-outs, reducing the number of players participating in this set piece and implementing rehearsed ploys to help them to continue to win and secure possession.

Regardless of the juncture of the game and the amount of time already played, every player must be capable of continuing his involvement to make an important and effective contribution to the performance of his unit and team by fulfilling his role successfully. Because of the nature of the game, every player is relied upon by others to perform a particular skill, whether during the restarts of play at line-outs, scrummages, kick-offs and drop-outs, or during the continual attacking or defending periods of the transitional passages of play.

There is also a great deal of running during a game, involving all players in movement around the field, executing a variety of skills and technical expertise at particular junctures, as well as supporting team-mates in attack and covering in defence. Players must have the necessary levels of physical fitness, conditioning and endurance to be capable of moving quickly from one particular play to another to effectively contribute to the team performance.

Close support running is a demanding feature of rugby football that requires high levels of physical fitness because it is essential that players are able to take advantage of every opportunity that occurs during open play. The speed, number and personal qualities of the support players in close proximity to the ball carrier when movements break down also affect the decision whether to ruck or maul the ball when a player is tackled in possession.

For example, the team that have more players arriving quickly at the point of the breakdown to achieve a numerical advantage over their opponents can positively influence the play for their team-mates' benefit. This is because they should be able to drive their opponents backwards and do one of the following things:

1 retain and secure possession to provide continuity in their attack and exploit any possible opportunity that develops
2 dispossess the opposing ball carrier to recover possession in a possibly advantageous field position, or

3 earn the advantage of the put-in to the scrummage should the referee decide to blow the whistle to end the passage of play and insist on the game being restarted with a set piece.

Individual players

The application and exhibition of individual skills must endorse and complement the tactical approach and not conflict with team-work or negate the agreed game plan and the practised repertoire of set moves and ploys. Within the framework of the team strategy, the coach should cater for the talented individual players to apply their skills when the appropriate opportunity presents itself. Regular participation in match-related practices under conditions controlled by the coach helps players to familiarise themselves with one another and learn individual preferences to perform certain actions in particular situations. Being able to anticipate the movements of team-mates gives every team an advantage over their opponents that they should attempt to exploit, develop and benefit from. Such attention to detail improves individual, unit and, consequently, team performances and achievements.

During their formative years, players need to experience both success and failure to appreciate the benefit of good tactical application, developing an ability to discern between appropriate options and implementing the correct and most suitable strategies and ploys. The learning process must incorporate both disappointment and euphoria, with the coach and players able to develop good tactical awareness, application, enterprise and endeavour to improve their performance.

The most influential players

All the players are required to make a worthwhile and valuable contribution to the performance of their particular unit and to the cohesion of the team. However, some players, because of the functional requirements of their position, have more responsibilities than others. Therefore the contribution of players in certain positions can be considered to be more crucial, as their efforts and decision making can affect the overall team performance.

For example, the captain's role is very important during the game, controlling the enthusiasm of the players, focusing their attention, helping them to maintain concentration, and applying their efforts to perform to the agreed game plan and basic pattern of play. The decisions made by the captain during the game are crucial because they influence the performance of the key decision makers, perhaps limiting or determining the selection of the available options.

The majestic Serge Blanco (France) has demonstrated throughout his illustrious career that enterprising and unexpected play complements a structured tactical approach

The other important players are the hooker, number eight, scrum-half, ly-half and the goal-kicker. During the game, each of these players has an mportant contribution to make to the team's achievements and tactical ipplication. The hooker and scrum-half are responsible for the correct lelivery of the ball when feeding the set pieces of line-outs and scrummages. The number eight controls the quality of the ball supplied to the scrum-half, vho in turn is also responsible for the distribution of the ball to the hreequarters. The half-back unit normally share the important esponsibility as the key decision makers, controlling the use of possession, vith the scrum-half marshalling the forwards' efforts and the fly-half :onducting the attacking and defensive efforts of the threequarters.

A reliable, consistently accurate and successful place kicker is also a valuable asset to and an important member of any team, because of his

A reliable place kicker is an asset to any team

ability to score points regularly. Care needs to be taken in selecting the player given the responsibility of taking the place kicks at goal because he should also be a capable player with the skills to successfully fulfil the demands of his playing position. Although the value of a good goal-kicker cannot be stressed enough, the player must earn selection on overall playing ability, contributing an effective performance as a successful and respected team member. In deciding upon the team formation, the selection committee should be unanimous about the tremendous importance and significance of the inclusion of a recognised and reliable goal-kicker because games can be won by a team successfully converting penalty kick and conversions.

Individual and unit playing positions

The playing positions in rugby football are so specific that each player requires particular physical attributes, qualities and abilities for him to function effectively and successfully in his chosen position. The techniques and skills are so specific to each position that players are very dependent on each other and rely heavily on their team-mates executing certain movements in a capable and proficient manner during particular phases of play.

The individual performances can determine the outcome of the whole team effort because, like a chain, the team can only be as successful as its weakest link. The most important factor is that players are familiar with the playing requirements of their position and capable of competing directly against an opponent for their team's benefit. Contained in the following chapters is a précis of the playing requirements and specific functions of each position.

2 The threequarters

The threequarters are a combination of players who need to be very competent in the performance of the basic, individual skills of passing, kicking, tackling and elusive running. This composite unit of players have the responsibility for the productive and effective use of the hard-earned possession secured by the forwards. During a game situation these players confront numerous situations when they are required to execute their playing skills and demonstrate the quality of their decision-making capabilities.

The basic objective of the threequarters is to turn possession into points, and this is achieved by utilising the ball purposefully at pace to keep opponents under pressure from every position and source of possession around the field.

Many diverse factors affect the performances of the threequarters as individuals and a cohesive unit, including:

the source of possession
the quality and speed of the ball presented to the scrum-half
the deployment and alignment of the players within the unit compared to their opponents
the accuracy, quality and timing of the passes
the speed of thought and competence of the important decision-making players in accurately assessing the playing situations and developing circumstances to make the correct decisions to utilise possession of the ball
the speed and abilities of the players to respond correctly to the demands of different attacking and defending situations
the lines of running of the players
the defensive strategy and individual capabilities of the participants, and
the fitness levels of the players involved, which determines their physical contribution and their concentration.

The seven threequarter positions are a combination of several smaller units operating together to produce an effective division capable of creating and exploiting attacking opportunities, as well as pressurising, restricting and frustrating the efforts of their opponents. The units that exist in the threequarters are as follows:

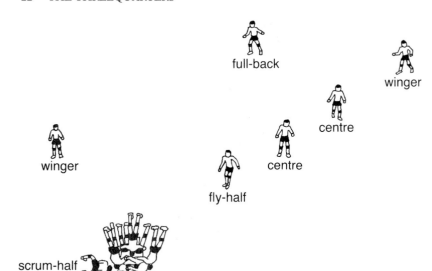

Solid and effective scrummaging by the forwards allows the threequarters to launch their attacks from deep positions

a The half-backs are normally the important decision makers, providing the link between the forwards and the rest of the threequarters.
b The fly-half and the centres are the inside midfield trio of players whose passing and running skills in attack determine the effectiveness of the transfer and delivery of the ball along the threequarter line to create time and space for their team-mates. During all phases of play these players must function as a defensive trio to restrict the efforts and available options of the opposing threequarters and prevent them from progressing beyond the gain line in possession of the ball.
c The centres work together as a pair, continually supporting the play of the half-backs, for example chasing kicks ahead to pressurise and attempt to unsettle and limit the efforts of the receiving player.
d The full-back and the wingers share the responsibilities of the last line of defence, with the full-back co-ordinating and controlling the deployment of the wingers to cover space, field kicks and perform covering tackles.

The basic principles of successful threequarter play, whether performed by an individual or resulting from a collective effort by the players, are:

1 to progress beyond the gain line when in possession
2 to support the player in possession to maintain the continuity of play

Falling away from the direction of the intended pass of the ball

3 the continual assessment of developing situations and the awareness to create and exploit attacking and counter-attacking opportunities
4 to pressurise opponents into making handling or decision-making errors and attempting to prevent them from crossing the gain line.

The full back

The modern game has altered the traditional role of this player considerably, developing the requirements and demands of the position from a simple custodian and last line of defence to include the duties of an inspirational and effective attacking player. The full-back's performance can prove very influential on the development and eventual outcome of a game.

The skills required by this player include the abilities to:

1 anticipate the intentions of the team in possession and assume good field positions to limit the space available for the opposition to exploit by kicking the ball
2 be courageous under the pressure of the high kick, catching the ball safely to recover, secure and utilise possession appropriately
3 be a good, solid and tenacious tackler
4 be a useful and effective kicker of the ball.

The developments in the role of the full-back focus on the player's abilities to exploit space and link up with wingers and support other members of the threequarter line. The full-back should be confident to launch attacks from deep positions when the ball has been kicked

The unpredictable and exciting David Campese (Australia) possesses the range of attacking and defensive skills needed by a successful winger

inaccurately by the other team and to enter the threequarter line to good effect when the ball has been won and secured in good attacking positions. This player needs to have a tremendous understanding of the game and the ability to anticipate and move into position to counter the intentions of the opposing threequarters, particularly the half-backs.

The wingers

The wingers are no longer simply the fastest players, able to catch a ball when running at speed and race away from the covering defence to finish off passing movements and score a try. Their role has been extended considerably to incorporate the added defensive duties of an auxiliary full-back. Wingers must now be very competent ball players with all the necessary skills to support the full-back in defence to prevent opponents from scoring, as well as the ability to catch the high and diagonally kicked ball and relieve the pressure with an effective and well-executed kick.

The wingers and full-back are now often involved in many passing movements and ploys at various times during the game, attempting to surprise the opposition by entering into the threequarter line at different points, to create or break through a gap to breach the defensive formation and cross the gain line or create an overlap situation.

The centres

The centres are probably the hardest workers in the threequarters, unselfishly and continuously running in support of the ball carrier and chasing the kicks of their half-backs to pressurise the defence and play all their team-mates on-side. The centres are also required to run back and support the full-back or wingers when the opposition have kicked the ball, to help to defend their line, or launch and support counter-attacks to exploit any available opportunities.

Centres need to develop very good ball-handling skills, with the ability to catch and pass the ball in one running stride. This quick and accurate transference of possession can help to create tremendous attacking opportunities for the player receiving the ball because of the extra space available for him to exploit.

The centres are also required to develop good contact skills, with the ability to perform the full range of effective tackling techniques to halt their opponents' advances, as well as the strength and skills to resist the challenges of the other team attempting to recover possession in the tackle.

Players in this position need to possess the skills to complement one another and the abilities of their fly-half: the deftness to transfer the ball quickly and accurately, the competence to kick the ball with both feet, the proficiency to assess developments, as well as the expertise and elusive running skills to exploit any attacking opportunities and thwart the other team's efforts when they are in possession of the ball.

The half-backs

These players are the decision makers directly responsible for their team's strategic and tactical performance. The half-backs decide when and where to execute particular ploys that determine the effectiveness of their team's use of the ball. The scrum-half is responsible for directing the efforts of the forwards and the fly-half is the leader of the threequarters. Both need to be inspirational players with a good understanding of the game and the abilities to assess situations quickly and correctly and respond accordingly for their team's benefit. The success, speed and distance of the link between the half-backs can be extremely influential on their team's performance, and these players need to work hard together during practice to develop a good rapport and understanding.

The fly-half

This player must be capable of performing competently under pressure and enjoy the responsibilities of the key decision maker. The fly-half needs to be able to analyse every playing position very quickly and select an appropriate ploy to exploit the situation. The fly-half also controls his team's defensive strategy, leading and directing players into positions that limit the options available for the other team. To achieve all these playing requirements, this player must be a good communicator who has earned the respect and appreciation of team-mates by demonstrating a tremendous understanding of the game, as well as a dextrous range of handling, running, kicking and tackling skills.

The scrum-half

The scrum-half provides the important link between the forwards and the threequarters, responsible for the feed of the scrummages and the distribution of the ball once possession has been secured from the set piece and transitional phases of play. This player must be able to transfer the ball under pressure and to deliver a quick and accurate pass to the fly-half. Should possession be slow or untidy, the scrum-half must decide whether to transfer the ball to the threequarters, attack close to the source and rely on the support of other players, or kick the ball to improve the territorial position and expose the deficiencies of the opposition defensive cover. This player must always be alert and adaptable, to exploit any attacking opportunity that develops during play. The scrum-half also needs to be confident, strong and courageous, to resist the challenges of the opposing forwards and tackle them when they are driving forwards in possession.

The threequarters in attack

The source, quality and speed of the possession considerably determines the threequarters' attacking options. Other influential factors include the field position, the deployment of players from both teams and the state of play at that particular moment in the game. All these criteria affect the decision of how to effectively utilise the ball to the team's benefit. In attack, the main purpose of every team is to continuously impose unrelenting pressure on their opponents to breach their defensive formation and score points. Achieving this objective requires players to select, implement and execute the most appropriate and effective ploys.

Making the key decisions is the responsibility of the half-backs, captain and possibly the leader of the forwards. These players between them can influence the pattern of play during a game and the tactical developments concerning the use of possession. The captain is responsible for making key decisions at stoppages in play, when the referee has whistled to penalise a player for infringing the laws of the game. The method of restarting the match will be determined by the type of penalty awarded by the referee, the field position and the state of play. The captain must consider the possibilities of the most appropriate action to respond to the circumstances. For example, it could be advantageous to consider a kick or drop-kick attempt at goal, providing the posts are in range of the kicker. However, this would prove an unsatisfactory and unsuitable option if there is a difference of more than three points in the scores between the two teams and there is only a minute of playing time remaining.

The success of the forward drive and the instructions of the scrum-half determine the release of the ball to the half-backs to control the possession won and secured from the set pieces of scrummages and line-outs, as well as from the transitional phases of the rucks and mauls. The priority for these players must be to keep their team moving forwards and progressing towards their opponents' goal line. This can be achieved through accurate kicking of the ball to improve field position or executing a passing movement in an attempt to progress beyond the gain line and breach the opposing threequarters' defensive formation.

With any passing movement the most important factors are:

1 communication among the players to ensure that everyone is prepared for the execution of a particular ploy
2 the alignment and deployment of players
3 the timing and speed of the execution of each individual assignment within the play
4 the lines of running
5 the accuracy of the pass, and
6 the number of players in support.

Many teams rehearse a selection of set ploys that they can execute from certain positions from a particular source of possession. The coach should work with the players to perfect a repertoire of ploys that they are capable of performing successfully from any source of possession or field position. It is sound organisation and individual player discipline that are crucial factors in ensuring the successful execution of these passing ploys.

There are numerous passing ploys that can be practised and included in the threequarters' repertoire once they have been perfected. The most appropriate for each team can vary depending on the skills and individual strengths of the players involved. Innovative thinking can result in the implementation of an enterprising repertoire of many passing ploys that can prove effective for the threequarters when in possession, taking advantage of certain field positions and playing circumstances to help to create scoring opportunities.

The limiting factor that determines the number of ploys included in the repertoire is the effectiveness and efficiency of the threequarters executing the movements. The standard ploys that most teams include in their repertoire include the switch/scissors pass, dummy scissors pass, loop pass and the miss moves. The success of these passing moves is determined by the quality and assurance of the performances of the players involved and the preceding use of possession.

Establishing an early attacking pattern of play with the threequarters exhibiting their intentions to utilise the possession, results in the opposing team adopting a suitable defensive pattern to counter their efforts. There are three basic attacking options:

1 transferring the ball quickly from the source of possession by lateral passing in an attempt to attack the space on the wings
2 using close interpassing movements that bring the ball back towards the forwards to commit all the defenders into a second-phase contest of the ruck or maul situation, or
3 kicking the ball into space keeping it close to the touchlines, in the centre of the field or diagonally across the field to improve the territorial position, keeping the forwards moving towards the opponents' goal line and maintaining pressure on the other team.

Once the defence have organised their deployment of players to counter the initial pattern of play, the tactical awareness and enterprise of the threequarters will determine the responses of their team attempting to extend and develop their strategy to expose the new areas of weakness. The many rehearsed passing ploys can be executed to alter the point of attack, vary the pattern of play and exploit the available space to the benefit of the team in possession.

Passing ploys for an attacking repertoire

The simplest passing movements performed to perfection at pace prove the most successful, effective and rewarding. It is possible to vary each of the following ploys to utilise the specific individual skills of particular players in the threequarter unit.

Attacking close to the source of possession.
The half-backs can take the collective or individual responsibility for attacking close to the source of possession. Teams often concentrate on the narrow or short side of the field, either kicking or running with the ball into space. However, a team can experiment with passing ploys that alter the direction of the movement to attack close to the source of possession on the open side of the field. The half-backs can link up with a number of supporting players including the full-back, blind-side winger, inside centre and back row forwards to expose any defensive weaknesses on either side of the field.

Ploy 1 The scrum-half receives the ball and breaks close to the source of possession, to attract the attention of the defending flanker covering the narrow side of the field, before transferring the ball to the support player. The close support could consist of the blind-side winger only, or could include the fly-half, centre and full-back, depending on the field position and the amount of space available on the short side.

Ploy 2 One of the forwards breaks with the ball to commit the fringing defender, before passing to the scrum-half or directly to the blind side winger. The player receiving possession can then receive support from the player missed out with the pass and possibly from the full-back and other forwards.

Ploy 3 The scrum-half flicks a short pass to the fly-half, blind-side winger or full-back advancing at pace and very close to the source of possession, attempting to run inside the breaking defensive cover before transferring the ball to one of the support players.

The England forwards have committed their opponents to the maul before transferring the ball to scrum-half Richard Hill to distribute to the three-quarters

Ploy 4 The scrum-half breaks wide from the source of possession and switches the direction of play by executing a scissors pass with the blind-side winger who either breaks through the defensive cover or sets up a ruck or maul situation. Once this ploy has been executed, the same players can perform a dummy scissors pass, with the scrum-half retaining the ball to attack the space along the touchline.

Ploy 5 The scrum-half transfers the ball to the fly-half, who delays the pass to allow time for either:

1 one of the centres to take a short or switch pass to straighten the angle of the attack and return with the ball close to the source of possession, or
2 one of the wingers to take a short pass inside the fly-half to alter the angle of the attack and penetrate the space behind the drifting cover defenders.

Ploy 6 The scrum-half pretends to pick up the ball from the feet of the number eight and breaks from the base of the scrummage in a crouched, driving position, giving the impression of carrying the ball close to the chest. The intention of this rather devious ploy is for the scrum-half to act as a decoy to encourage the opposing flanker to break from the scrummage,

iving the forwards in control of the ball a numerical advantage to help them
o successfully execute a secondary drive to advance towards their
opponents' goal line. This ploy could also result in a penalty being awarded
o the team in possession, should the scrum-half's performance convince the
opposing flanker to advance into an off-side position and attempt to tackle
he supposed ball carrier.

Ploy 7 One of the half-backs kicks the ball high into the space on the narrow
side of the field and behind the covering blind-side winger. The attacking
winger follows the ball to play all the forwards on-side, and all the
supporting players attempt to impose as much pressure as possible on the
defender having to turn and chase backwards to recover the ball. The
support players advance quickly to restrict the number of options available
for the defending team to utilise and benefit from the possession.

*It is vitally important that the forwards protect their scrum-half, thereby creating a physical
barrier and blocking the efforts of their opponents attempting to regain possession*

Attacking in the centre of the field

Creating and exploiting space in the centre of the field is probably the mos difficult way to attack successfully from first phase possession o scrummages and line-outs, because of the sound organisation of th defending unit of threequarters. However, it is possible to breach th defensive cover by performing passing ploys that involve quick thinking deception and good handling skills, incorporating the elusive- and incisive running abilities of the threequarters to alter the angle and direction of th attack.

Ploy 1 The fly-half transfers the ball with a short pass to the inside centr who runs straight to check and commit the drifting defenders, including th back-row forwards, and set up a ruck or maul situation.

Ploy 2 The miss moves are very successful ploys for quickly transferring th ball away from the source of possession. Executing these passing ploy efficiently at pace can create and exploit space either in the centre or on th wide areas of the field, depending on the selection and implementation o the particular ploy:

1 the fly-half missing the inside centre with the pass and transferring the ba to either the outside centre or directly to the full back running into th threequarter line
2 the inside centre missing the outside centre with the pass and transferrin the ball directly to the full back running into the line
3 the pass missing the outside centre and being transferred directly to th winger with the full-back supporting on the outside of the line, or
4 the fly-half missing out both centres with the pass and distributing the ba directly to either the winger or the full back.

Ploy 3 The ball is distributed to the fly-half and transferred to the insid centre while they are moving slowly; it is then passed to the full-back entering the threequarter line running very straight and at tremendous pace The full-back will be able to transfer the ball to the threequarters supportin on both the outside and inside of the run, to exploit any space that th sudden injection of pace creates.

Ploy 4 This is a variation of the above ploy, with the open side winge entering the threequarter line between the centres to alter the angle of th attack and exploit the drifting of the defensive players.

Ploy 5 The scrum-half breaks from the source of possession, runnin straight across the field, and either:

1 offers the ball to the fly-half with a dummy switch pass before transferrin a short pass to the inside centre running straight, or

2 repeats the same actions but transfers the ball directly to the outside centre or full-back, missing out the inside centre with the pass.

Ploy 6 The ball is transferred via the half-backs to the inside centre who performs a scissors pass with the outside centre, full-back or blind-side winger to alter the direction of the attack.

Ploy 7 The fly-half loops around the inside centre to receive a return pass before transferring the ball with a short pass to either the outside centre, blind-side winger or full-back running straight, quickly altering the angle of the attack to wrong-foot and penetrate the defensive cover.

Ploy 8 On receiving the ball, the fly-half, in conjunction with the inside centre, slightly drifts across the field, attempting to encourage the defending players to cover the outside break or an attack wide out. The outside centre then runs behind the two players and executes a scissors movement with the fly-half. The intention is to commit the opposing defenders to the tackle and involve them in a ruck or maul situation close to the original source of possession, restricting the amount of covering players to counter the next attack.

Back row forwards Mike Teague and Peter Winterbottom are supported by scrum-half Richard Hill as they attack close to the scrummage and attempt to exploit the lack of defensive cover

Ploy 9 One of the inside trio of players chip kicks the ball over the advancing threequarters to exploit the space immediately behind them and in front of the full-back.

Ploy 10 The fly-half or inside centre kicks a very high ball towards the full-back, with both centres and as many other support players as possible following the kick to pressurise the receiving player attempting to unsettle the confidence of the full-back.

Ploy 11 When the play is concentrated around the opponents' 22-metre area and in a relatively central position in the field, one of the half-backs or threequarters can attempt a drop kick at goal to earn three points for his team.

Attacking the wide positions

Moving the ball quickly to the wingers to exploit their pace, elusive-running skills and the supporting capabilities of the other team members constitutes a strategy for attacking the space on the edges of the playing area. The most obvious method of transferring the ball to the wingers is using the quick passing skills of the scrum-half and the inside trio of players. However there are variations that involve the miss moves previously described above, deception to delay the covering defenders, and the inclusion of the full-back in the threequarter line.

Ploy 1 The ball is transferred as quickly as possible from the scrum-half to the fly-half, who has marshalled the threequarters to stand in deep positions to provide enough time and space for the ball to be transferred accurately to the winger. Either the blind-side winger or the full back can be involved and enter the line of threequarters at various points, to attract the defending team's attention and create space for the winger on the outside.

The wingers must also be capable of distributing the ball while running at full speed to players running in support, and making the ball available when tackled, to help to maintain the momentum of the attack. Keeping the ball in play intensifies the pressure on opponents and stretches their defensive cover. When the support players are slow to arrive and the winger is in danger of being isolated, the cross kick is a useful and effective ploy to continue an attacking movement. Kicking the ball across the field alters the point of the attacking thrust, and thereby exploits any available space and keeps the ball in play to benefit from the arrival of the support players.

Ploy 2 After receiving the ball the outside centre executes a switch pass with the winger, who immediately performs a second switch pass with the inside centre; this player is running wide to link up with the supporting full-back and the other threequarters looping around to support the ball carrier on the outside.

Ploy 3 The centres deceptively extend the distance between themselves when possession is secured to allow the full-back to enter the threequarter line at pace and transfer the ball to the outside centre and winger running in support.

Ploy 4 The fly-half stands on the narrow side of the field but the scrum-half delivers the ball:

1 directly to the fly-half, full-back or blind-side winger running to the open side of the field
2 to the fly-half, who receives the ball standing still and delivers a long pass to the inside centre or full-back running forwards on the open side of the field. Should the centre receive the ball, the full-back supports this ploy by entering the line at any of the positions outside this player.

The numerical advantage created by the deceptive positioning of the fly-half can be exploited by the quick transference of the ball along the line to the open-side winger.

Ploy 5 Varying the above ploy, the fly-half runs towards the narrow side of the field but the scrum-half delivers the ball directly to the blind-side winger or the full-back, who are running across the source of possession to the open side to link up with the remainder of the waiting threequarters.

Ploy 6 The fly-half or inside centre kicks the ball diagonally behind the approaching threequarters, beyond the defending open-side winger and away from the cover positioning of the full-back, for the attacking winger to chase and pressurise the recovering defenders.

The threequarters in defence

Good defensive play involves players attempting to nullify the advantage of the team in possession by exerting the maximum amount of continuous and controlled pressure on their opponents, limiting the amount of time and space and consequently the attacking options available. The immediate objective of defending players should be to prevent the ball carrier from crossing the gain line, halting his progress at the tackle line. The defending unit should also attempt to persuade and encourage the attacker to execute a particular action that the defensive unit are prepared to counter and suppress.

Strategies in a defending repertoire

Defending against a team running with the ball

There are two different defensive strategies for the threequarters to employ when the other team have possession of the ball:

1 the players are directly responsible for tackling or shadowing their opposite number to restrict their contribution, or
2 the players defend specific, channelled areas of the field and drift across the pitch to cover the next zone when the ball has been transferred from their channel.

There are advantages and disadvantages of adopting either strategy; the coach and threequarters must decide the more suitable one to perform from every playing scenario.

One-to-one defence The one-to-one defence, in which players are directly responsible for their opposite number, exerts greater pressure on opponents and is an effective defensive strategy when the other team are receiving the ball slowly from the sources of possession. At scrummages, rucks and mauls the defending unit of threequarters are able to limit the amount of space available by standing behind the feet of their forwards involved in the ball-winning situation. As a result the defenders can pressurise the players in possession behind the gain line, providing the fly-half and centres advance quickly as a controlled unit. The defender nearest the source of possession should lead the advance, with the other two players in the defensive line staggered slightly behind.

Channel or zone defence The channel or zone defence can be used at a line-out situation or when the attacking players supporting the ball carrier outnumber the defenders. The purpose of this defensive strategy is to maintain a line of players between the ball carrier and the try line, delaying the direct forward progress of the attacker and attempting to isolate this player from the available support. To achieve this objective the threequarters cover backwards and drift across the field, preventing the attacking player from breaching the defensive formation on the outside. The defensive players also try to encourage the attacking player to attempt an inside break to breach the blanket coverage of the threequarters by running infield, so that he can be tackled by the defensive reinforcements.

Overlap situations Occasions arise when the attacking team have managed to create an overlap situation in which they have more players in support of the ball carrier than there are defenders. The minimum overlap is a two-against-one situation, with the attacking team enjoying the advantage of the extra player. The defender has the problem of attempting to delay the tackers' progress and creating doubt in the mind of the player in ossession about the selection and execution of the most effective option to xploit the situation. The defending player must attempt to seize the iitiative by confusing the ball carrier with a series of conflicting actions, etreating away from the ball carrier and feigning to advance towards the tackers. The objective of these actions, delaying a commitment to the ackle, will also help to create more time for the covering defenders to reach ie crisis area and support the isolated defender.

Obviously the attacking players will continue to progress forwards with ie ball, and sometimes the cover will not be able to reach the isolated efender in time to support these delaying tactics. Therefore at some point ie defender will have to decide on the most suitable course of action to limit ie attacking players' achievements.

The options available for the defensive player involve:

delaying further and retaining a central position between the two ttackers, attempting to force the ball carrier to run inside towards the overing defenders

tackling the ball carrier, attempting to halt the progress of the player in ossession and prevent the successful transfer of the ball to the support ayers, or

attempting to anticipate the exact timing and execution of the pass and revent its completion by intercepting the ball as the attacking player ttempts to transfer possession to the support player.

Many coaches and players insist that the last defender pressurises the ball arrier by attempting to tackle him to halt the progress of the attack. Obviously this is the safest option because in theory a successful tackle will reak down the movement; however, the defending player should never rule ut the devastating effect that can be achieved from a successful iterception. Recovering possession by intercepting the pass can nmediately change the course of the game, turning a defensive situation ito an attacking one, with a great opportunity to exploit the lack of cover in ie opponents' defensive formation.

Although the results of intercepting the pass can prove very rewarding for ie defender, this action is also a high-risk ploy and an unsuccessful attempt an make the player look extremely foolish, exposing the goal line for the ttacking players to score an uncontested try. Therefore the defender must uickly assess the developing situation to select and execute the most ppropriate and effective tactic in an attempt to prevent the attacking layers from being rewarded with a score.

Defending against a team kicking the ball

The threequarters must also practise retreating quickly to support the efensive actions of the full-back and wingers when the ball is kicked over their heads. The attacking players are at an immediate advantage because they are expecting the execution of the intended ploy, unlike the defending team, who must advance towards their opposite number to pressurise their opponents before turning around to chase the kick and support the rearguard action of their defensive triumvirate.

Because of the size of the playing area and the deployment of the players there is often a great deal of space available for the attacking team to exploit. Good positioning by the full-back and the wingers can limit the space available, but good opportunities will always exist for a well-directed and executed kick to successfully pressurise defences and consequently improve the attacking team's territorial position.

The defensive strategies that players covering the kick ahead can implement depend on several factors:

1 the accuracy of the kick ahead
2 the field position and intended landing area of the ball
3 the number and formation of the attacking players chasing the kick
4 the playing abilities, competence and confidence of the player fielding the kick, and
5 the speed of the retreating players to move into good support positions to help to launch effective counter-attacks.

The accuracy and distance of the kick is obviously an important factor. For example, the ball kicked high but too far forwards into the defending 22-metre area can easily be caught by one of the covering players. Depending on the amount of pressure exerted by the chasing players, the defender can either exploit the amount of space available or catch the ball standing still and call for a 'Mark', in an attempt to temporarily halt the flow of play. Providing the execution of this ploy conforms with the laws of the game, the referee will award the mark, stopping the play to allow the remainder of the defending team to retreat behind the ball before the player restarts the match by kicking the ball through the mark.

Defending with possession

Options available to the defender when the ball is safely fielded and possession is securely collected are as follows.

a He can launch a counter-attack to exploit the situation by:
1 running towards the area that contains the majority of team-mates to recruit their help and support
2 attacking the available spaces and relying on team-mates to arrive quickly in support to continue the progress of the movement, or
3 utilising the supporting players to execute switch or dummy switch moves to deceive and delay the advancing opponents, attempting to confuse them about the intended direction of the counter-attack.

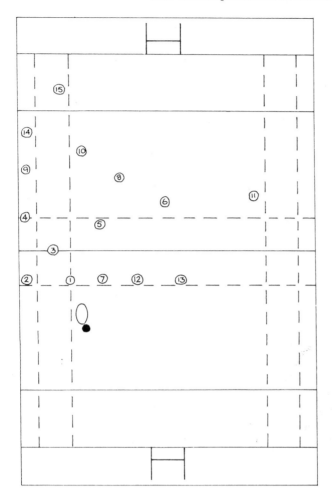

Covering the field to defend against opponents opting to kick the ball into touch from a penalty award

b He can kick the ball:
   1 safely into touch, either directly or along the ground, to conform with the requirements of the laws of the game, or
   2 high and accurately with the intention that the ball remains inside the playing area. The defending player chases the kick ahead to play team-mates on-side and recruit their support to pressurise the opposing player who is fielding possession.

   Whether or not the most effective option is executed depends on the players' abilities to assess the situation and make the appropriate decision to successfully restrict the achievements of the opponents. Players must always be prepared to respond quickly to the developing situations and capable of exploiting any opportunity that presents itself as a result of their defensive actions.

Defending inside the 22-metre area

When play progresses inside a team's 22-metre area, they need to have confidence in their collective and individual abilities to relieve the pressure at the earliest opportunity, improving their territorial position by either running with the ball or kicking it into touch further down the field. Before the defending team are capable of improving their field position they must first win possession from the set pieces or transitional phases of play.

During these forward contests, the threequarters must implement an effective defensive strategy to prevent their opponents from scoring should they secure possession in such a good attacking position. From every phase of play each player must be aware of his individual responsibility. Inside the 22-metre area the half-backs and full-back are the most important defenders because their actions determine the defensive formation and strategy to maintain a resolute defence. During the set pieces either the fly-half or full-back must stand in a deep position to receive the ball from the scrum-half and then perform a relieving kick into touch.

To cover the possibility that the defending team do not win possession, the player not expecting to receive the ball must assume responsibility to lead the threequarter line and apply as much pressure as possible on the opposing players, attempting to prevent any ball carrier from crossing the tackle or gain line. The player standing in the deep position must also cover across the field to support and contribute towards the defensive strategy when possession is lost.

(Right) *The forwards harness their individual strength and skills into a powerful and cohesive unit to compete for possession during all phases of play*

3 The forwards

n all phases of competition the forwards must be prepared for physical onfrontation and capable of answering the challenge with a controlled and ggressive approach. During participation in the first-phase contests for ossession – the scrummages, line-outs and kick-offs – it is important that ne forwards are aware of their individual roles in their contribution to the nit. During the transitional phases of play – the rucks and mauls – the orwards must be very mobile around the field and quick to the breakdown f attacks, capable of assessing where their contribution would prove the nost effective for their team, to help to retain and secure possession while reventing their opponents from achieving the same.

The playing positions of the forwards at the scrummages are a collection f smaller units that bind tightly together to form a powerful combination to in, secure and channel the ball to the scrum-half. The different units are as ollows.

The front row

Front-row players improve their craft, performance and achievement wit
maturity and experience of playing their position. There are so man
peculiar requirements and intricacies involved in these combative position
that practical knowledge is the vital key to success. They are the mos
directly confrontational participants in the game; their actions during pla
are often considered intimidatory to unsettle opponents.

There are three specific positions in the front row: the loose-head prop
tight-head prop and the hooker. The props are aptly named because thei
most important role is in supporting the scrummages, establishing a soli
platform and foundation for the forward unit. The front-row forwards nee
to be naturally strong, with a squat and stocky physique. The demands of th
position – the supporting, twisting and turning – require these players t
have strong backs, to help to transfer and direct the weight and drive of a
the other forwards involved in this set piece.

Because the front row form the basis of the scrummage, they must b
tightly bound together. Both props place their arms around the waist of th
hooker, who binds over the top of the props' shoulders. The props need

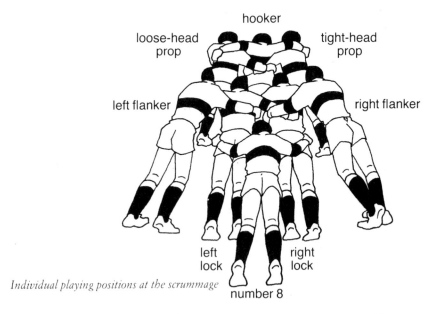

Individual playing positions at the scrummage

wide, solid base, and their feet positions are very important. To ensur
greater stability it is necessary for each prop to place his outside foot in fror
of the inside foot, helping to keep his hips below the level of his shoulder:
Also, the loose-head needs to create the beginning of the channel for th
hooker to direct the ball backwards and must assume a slightly wider stanc
than the tight-head.

The loose-head prop

The main purpose of the loose-head prop is to support the whole weight of the opposing tight-head plus the added strain of the pressure exerted by the supporting forwards. It is also the responsibility of the loose-head to keep the scrummage high enough for the scrum-half to feed the ball correctly into the tunnel between the two front rows and for the hooker to be able to observe the actions of the scrum-half.

The loose-head possibly needs to be the stronger of the two props, able to keep a straight back to absorb all the pressure of the drive exerted by the opposition and transmit the scrummaging power coming from behind into forward momentum.

The tight-head prop

This player also needs to be strong to help to support the hooker and transmit the drive of the other forwards to disrupt the opposition's efforts as much as possible. The tight-head prop needs the strength, ability and technique to scrummage lower than the loose-head to improve the hooker's view of the ball.

The hooker

Although the hooker's main responsibility during the scrummages is to strike for the ball and compete in a direct contest for possession, he must be able to alter position quickly to contribute to the forward drive. The preparation for the scrummage is therefore very important, with the hooker bound as closely and tightly to the props as possible. The hooker must be comfortably positioned, with the right foot unrestricted and poised to strike for the ball, and the left foot supporting the remainder of the body weight and helping to maintain good balance.

The hooker needs to try to gain every advantage that he can over his opposite number by lowering himself towards the ground. This can be successfully achieved by:

1 dropping his backside below the level of his shoulders, then moving his right foot closer to where the ball will be delivered by the scrum-half
2 twisting his shoulders towards the feeding scrum-half to improve his view and restrict his opponents' sight of the ball.

The hooker will improve the control and quality of the strike for the ball by using the inside of the right foot, guiding the ball backwards between the legs of the loose-head prop. Although a strike with the outside of the left foot can prove quicker, the depth of the strike is poor and the loose-head prop has to help to guide the ball backwards, which obviously affects the positioning of the feet and adversely affects the mechanics and forward momentum of the scrummage.

When the opposing team are putting the ball into the scrummage, the hooker must contribute to the forward drive of the snap shove when the ball enters the tunnel between the two front rows. On occasions it should be possible for the hooker to compete for the ball when the opposing scrum-half feeds the scrummage. Deciding to contest the strike should be a collective decision made by all the front-row players before the scrummage is formed, because these players need to alter their positioning and techniques.

The tight-head prop is the most important support player when the front row have decided to strike for the ball against the head, attempting to improve the hooker's view of the ball by lifting up the opposing loose-head prop. In driving underneath and lifting him up, the tight-head will also manage to increase the distance that the opposing hooker is positioned from the entrance to the tunnel and eliminate the majority of the advantage gained from the put-in of the ball. The tight-head should also close the tunnel once the ball enters the scrummage, by stepping across with the right foot to create a channel for the ball, and help to guide the ball backwards after a successful strike.

The second row

The lock forwards

It is important that the second-row players develop a good rapport and form a solid, balanced and complementary partnership, because they are required to work hard as a unit and generate as much forward momentum as possible during the scrummages. On some occasions the second-row forwards are required to lock the scrummage and prevent their opponents from establishing a forward drive. The most important factors contributing to the successful performance of these duties are:

1 tight binding on the prop forwards as well as one another
2 assuming the correct body position with a straight back, the head slightly tilted backwards and the eyes looking forwards, and
3 harnessing the powerful drive of their legs from a solid base.

Each of the lock forwards needs to be strong enough to alter his scrummaging position and thereby retain a sound mechanical position to compensate for any possible movements of the front-row players during this set piece. The binding of the lock forwards on the props is crucial in maintaining the drive without affecting the position or function of the players involved or the hooker. The technique of binding is peculiar to these playing positions and is a joint decision between the respective prop and the lock forward. The players have the choice to bind with:

1 the outside arm of each lock placed through the legs of the prop with the hand gripping the shirt and/or the top of the prop's shorts, or
2 the hand wrapped around the prop's inside leg to grip his shorts at hip level.

When the hooker intends to strike for the ball, the locks should be driving with their outside shoulder positioned on the uppermost part of the prop's thigh, with the point of contact below the buttock. The hooker should alter position after striking the ball, moving both feet backwards to enable the locks to utilise both shoulders in their forward drive.

The back row

The two flankers and the number eight are the three players who constitute the unit of the back row, often known as the breakaway forwards. This is a good term that accurately describes the general function of these positions during open play, when they are involved in covering tremendous distances at speed in an attempt to be the first forwards to the breakdown in the flow of play. However, at the scrummages these players are required to contribute their strength and power to drive forwards, helping to control the channel and distribution of the ball to the scrum-half.

All three back-row players must be capable of answering and enjoying the robust physical challenges that they continually encounter during their participation in competitive games. As well as the ability to compete in physical exchanges with tenacious tackling and commitment, these players must also be capable of demonstrating competent ball-handling and kicking skills, helping to initiate and support attacks and relieving the pressure when defending.

The number eight

This player has an important role to play in compacting the scrummage, controlling the channel and dictating the release of the ball to protect the scrum-half. The number eight is sometimes responsible for picking the ball out of the scrummage to relieve the pressure on the scrum-half and vary the use of possession. The rapport, communication and understanding between the number eight and scrum-half are vital factors that can determine the quality of possession and the performance of a team during a game.

Tactical ploys

There are numerous tactical ploys that can be practised and developed to form a repertoire of attacking moves initiated by the number eight:

Ploy 1 He requests an extra effort from the forwards to create a secondary drive to disrupt the efforts of the opposition. They carefully control the ball with the feet to exploit any advantage resulting from the extra forward momentum generated by the secondary drive. As well as the territorial gain, the forwards achieve a tremendous psychological boost over their opponents when they are able to execute a controlled and effective secondary drive at the scrummage.

Ploy 2 The number eight picks the ball out of the scrummage and gives a short pass to the scrum-half, improving the amount of time available and the quality of possession for the half-back.

Ploy 3 He links up with the flankers and the scrum-half, driving forwards with the ball to exploit any space close to the scrummage and create attacking opportunities.

Ploy 4 The number eight breaks laterally from the scrummage to receive a short pass from the scrum-half, and:

1 drives forwards to commit the opposing fly-half, or
2 acts as a pivot for the scrum-half to loop around and receive the return pass or use as a decoy, distributing the ball to the blind-side winger or centre running in the other direction and altering the spearhead of the attack.

Ploy 5 Moving across to the left to fill the gap between the lock and flanker, he is available to help to control and collect the ball directed down channel one. He picks up the ball to attack the space on the right side of the scrummage, with the immediate support of the right flanker and the following lock forwards breaking from the set piece. This ploy can prove very effective because it attacks the space close to the source of possession, with the spearhead of the attack directed away from the majority of the forwards involved in the scrummage.

The number eight also has another equally important role to perform at the scrummages when possession is lost and secured by the opposition, operating as part of an immediate defensive unit with the flankers and the scrum-half, to minimise their opponents' success. The defensive cover at the scrummages needs to be well organised, with each player aware of his responsibilities and capable of supporting his team-mates to limit the other team's achievements and prevent them from crossing the gain line.

The flankers

The flankers bind with their inside arm onto the side of the lock forwards, positioning their head on the outside hip of the prop in front of them, in a good driving position where they can also see into the tunnel and watch the ball enter the scrummage. On the opposition put-in, the nearer flanker is usually responsible for communicating with the other forwards and informing them when the ball has entered the tunnel, signalling an eight-man drive instead of the hooker attempting to strike for the ball.

The most effective scrummaging formation is 3–4–1, with both flankers binding on the props and contributing to the forward drive at the scrummages. The flankers should ensure that they are always aware of the position of the ball during the scrummages because they may be required to guide the ball across to the number eight to control and improve the quality of possession. To increase the number of attacking options, it may occasionally be worthwhile for the forwards to alter the style of the formation, with the number eight moving across to the left to bind onto the flanker and the lock forward. The right flanker also moves backwards and across to fill the number eight position and continue driving through the centre of the scrummage.

Scrummaging

During the scrummages the forwards are bound tightly together to compete in a direct physical contest with their opponents to win possession of the ball. The team responsible for the feed into the scrummage have a definite advantage over their opponents and one that they should exploit to maximum effect. The successes and failures of the forward unit at the scrummage have a tremendous psychological effect on the whole team because it is such an important source of primary, or first-phase, possession. The ability to secure good possession regularly at these set pieces, with the forwards in control of the ball, provides an excellent platform for the team to launch attacking ploys to exploit any available opportunities.

The decision-making players are able to positively influence a match's pattern of play when their forwards are regularly capable of winning and controlling good ball from their own solid and tight scrummaging. A forward unit capable of dominating their opponents at this set piece will enable their important decision makers to control the game because of the continuous supply of guaranteed possession.

Match analysis has highlighted the importance of the scrummage as an influential feature of rugby football: there are approximately 40 scrummages during a match played over 80 minutes. Participating in this competitive set piece is, physically and mentally, extremely demanding. The intensity of the contest requires tremendous levels of specific fitness, techniques and concentration. Therefore pressure exerted by the forwards at the scrummages can drain the strength and stamina of their opponents, which can severely limit their efforts around the field and their successes at securing possession at the other contests of line-outs, rucks and mauls.

Players and coaches should therefore devote time to acquiring the specific fitness and mastering the techniques required for successful participation at the scrummages. Specific scrummaging practices also help to develop good understanding, harnessing the efforts and application of the forward unit. However, although very important and influential, the coach and players should be careful that they do not place too much emphasis on scrummaging practice, to the detriment of developing the necessary individual and unit skills to win the ball at the other forward contests and sources of possession.

Attacking tactics at the scrummage
The snap shove
This is a controlled, co-ordinated and explosive drive achieved when the forwards pull together with their arms and straighten their legs as the ball enters the scrummage. The snap shove can be very effective in giving one hooker an advantage over the other because the unit are moving marginally

The combined effort of the seven forwards driving forwards, freeing the hooker to concentrate on striking for the ball

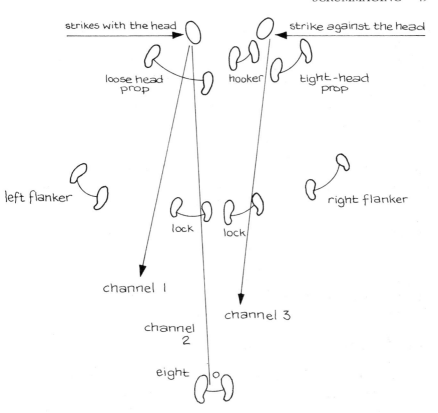

strikes with the head

strike against the head

loose head prop

hooker

tight-head prop

left flanker

right flanker

lock

lock

channel 1

channel 3

channel 2

eight

Foot positions of the forwards at the scrummage

forwards when the ball enters the scrummage. Every forward unit should be attempting to produce an effective snap shove at the scrummage to increase the pressure on their opponents and restrict the success of their efforts.

Before engaging the opposition, the forwards should prepare for the set-piece contest carefully and organise their playing personnel to good effect. The front-row players should be correctly bound together with the support of their second-row players, comprising two locks and both flankers, bound in a sound mechanical position ready to drive forwards when given the signal.

When the referee requests the two units of forwards to engage at the scrummage, the front row advance aggressively towards their opponents by taking one step and crouching into a low position. On contact the front row attempt to raise the height of their opponents to achieve an advantageous driving position.

Channelling the ball during the scrummages

Before the ball is put into the scrummage the participating players should be aware of their collective responsibilities for channelling the ball through their feet to the scrum-half. The players must position their feet carefully so that they are able to drive the scrummage forwards and leave clear channels for the ball to be directed through. Once the hooker has been successful in winning the strike of the ball and has guided it backwards through the legs of the loose-head prop, there are three recognised channels for the ball to be accurately directed through to the scrum-half.

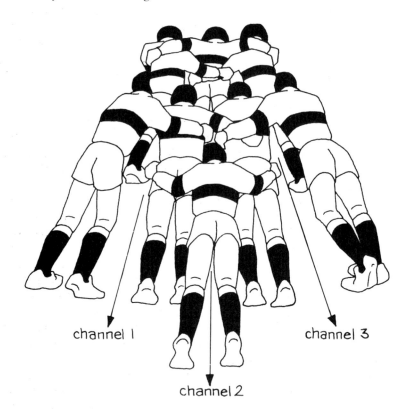

Channelling the ball at the scrummage

Channel one This allows the ball to emerge very quickly from the scrummage between the foot positions of the left flanker and lock forward.

Channel two This is a subtle variation of the above, requiring a deeper strike from the hooker to direct the ball backwards through the channel between the legs of the loose-head prop and the left lock forward towards the number eight, to slow down the delivery and improve the control of the ball.

Channel three This is reserved for the ball that is won by the hooker against the head, when the other team are putting in the ball to the scrummage. The ball is directed backwards by the hooker using the outside of the right foot, with extra support and guidance from the tight-head prop's left foot. Then the ball is deflected between the legs of the right lock forward to the feet of the number eight, who controls the use or delivery of the ball.

The secondary drive

The secondary drive is a useful and effective strategy to ensure that the unit of forwards winning possession at the scrummage are able to improve the channelling of the ball or exploit good field position and the supremacy of the forwards to progress towards their opponents' goal line and score a push-over try. This strategy can also disrupt the organisation of the opposition scrummage and improve the security and quality of possession being channelled.

The number eight must be a competent ball player because of the responsibility for initiating the drive, keeping the ball moving forwards under control and deciding how to use possession. The number eight has the option of picking up the ball to drive forwards over the gain line to commit the opposing scrum-half and back-row players as a rehearsed ploy, or accurately distributing the ball to the scrum-half.

To support the secondary drive and improve the effectiveness of the powerful surge forwards, other players from the threequarters are allowed to join the scrummage. When the set piece is close to the opponents' goal line this can prove a very effective tactic, helping to make sure that the scrummage maintains its forward momentum to cross over the goal line, with the ball under control, to score a try. In such good attacking field positions, the players expecting to join the threequarters in their attack would be the full-back and possibly the blind-side winger when the set piece is close to the touchline. These two players, supported by the scrum-half when necessary, could add their weight and driving power to the scrummage to improve the forward unit's progress.

Although this tactic can have a successful result, players must be sure that their contribution will prove decisive and that their forwards have won the ball at the set piece and are controlling the channel. Otherwise their actions could prove detrimental, disrupting the control to lose possession and provide their opponents with an excellent attacking opportunity because of the lack of defensive cover.

Locking the scrummage

When the forwards are at a physical disadvantage in competing against a heavier and stronger unit, the most important factor in scrummaging is damage limitation, attempting to prevent the opponents from exploiting their obvious advantages. A team under pressure at this particular set piece should attempt to counter their opponents' drive by locking the scrummage.

A good locking position during a scrummage: feet are splayed to increase the contact of the studs with the ground, legs are straight and the body is held rigid

The second-row and back-row players are mainly responsible for locking the scrummages by splaying their feet to improve the contact with the ground and keeping the legs straight from the hips by pushing back the knees.

It is almost impossible for the front-row players to contribute to the locking action of the other forwards in the scrummages. The props have to maintain a driving position to counter their opponents' power and transfer the drive of their team-mates, and the hooker must continue to strike for his own ball and direct it through channel one to avoid any delay in the ball travelling to the scrum-half.

Should the hooker manage to overcome the discomfort created by the pressure exerted by the stronger opposing forwards to win the ball and direct it backwards through channel two, the supporting forwards should attempt to transform their locked scrummage and initiate a forward drive to ensure that the ball reaches the number eight without too much delay.

Wheeling the scrummage

Wheeling the scrummage can prove an effective strategy to improve or restrict the attacking options by:

1 turning the defending forwards to create extra space and attacking opportunities, as well as improving the cover for the scrum-half, or
2 disrupting the quality of possession won by the other team and the attacking opportunities by initiating the wheel when the scrummage has been awarded to the opposition close to the right-hand touchline.

The laws of the game prevent the scrummage from being wheeled beyond 90 degrees, which means that a team must be able to control their efforts to apitalise on this strategy. To initiate a wheel at the scrummage, the loose-ead prop, left lock and number eight should concentrate on driving orwards with their left shoulder.

It is important that the team are prepared to counter the effects of the opposition wheeling the scrummage by rehearsing suitable strategies to limit he damage caused. There are a number of possible ploys that a team can nplement.

loy 1 They continue to wheel the scrummage beyond 90 degrees, for the eferee to stop the play and restart the set-piece contest.

loy 2 The forwards attempt to counter their opponents' initiation of a heel. For the efforts of the defensive unit to be successful, every player nust remain bound into the scrummage and contribute to the drive. The ght-head prop must be driven forwards, while the loose-head prop attempts to remain stationery and resist the efforts of the opposition attempting to wheel the scrummage.

loy 3 The number eight picks up the ball and:

quickly transfers possession to the scrum-half, who has moved backwards o benefit from the extra space
drives forwards, attempting to progress beyond the gain line to pressurise he opposition close to the scrummage and utilise the support of the flankers nd lock forwards.

loy 4 A secondary drive is initiated at the earliest opportunity to exploit the robability that one or more of the opposing players will have broken ackwards to assume a position close to the scrummage.

Defensive strategies at the scrummage

When a team fail to secure possession from the scrummage, the flankers are nitially required to defend the area close to the set piece and attempt to revent their opponents from progressing beyond the gain line. Once the crum-half has distributed the ball away from the area of the scrummage to he threequarters, the defensive duties of the flankers involve exerting as nuch pressure as possible on the opposing fly-half and threequarters by dvancing quickly to limit the space and attacking options available.

The flankers are responsible for exerting as much pressure as possible on he half-backs when their team have been unsuccessful in winning ossession of the ball at the scrummage. The first responsibility of the back-ow players is to devise a defensive strategy that deals with the opposition

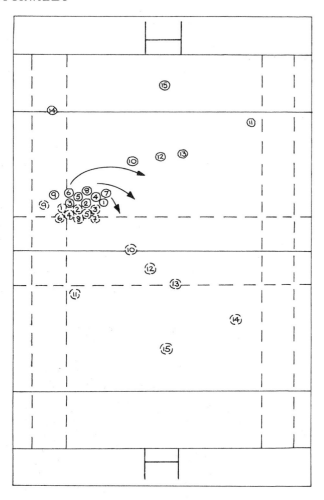

Back-row defence at the scrummage

scrum-half and back-row players breaking close to the set piece to attack an
exploit any space around the fringes of the scrummage.

A team winning possession at the scrummage will favour attacking on th
opposite side to the one from which the scrum-half feeds the ball into the se
piece. The most effective and straightforward defensive strategy when th
opposition win the ball from their own put-in requires the right flanker t
tackle the first player breaking from the set piece, with the number eigh
responsible for covering the actions of the support player. The defensiv
strategy and organisation for a team attempting to exploit the space on th
same side as they feed the ball into the scrummage should involve the scrum
half tackling the initial ball carrier, with either the left flanker or numbe
eight responsible for the support player.

When the scrum-half immediately distributes the ball to the threequarters, the defending back row must break forwards to pressurise the fly-half receiving the ball, to limit the time and number of attacking options available. Once the fly-half has transferred the ball along the threequarter line, the back row should continue running across the field to shepherd the movement of the interpassing players, remaining inside each player receiving the ball to cover and prevent the threequarters from attempting an inside break.

Each player in the threequarters is responsible for countering the actions of his opposite number, attempting to halt his advance when the player receives possession. In breaking towards the threequarters, the back-row players function as a unit supporting the defensive formation of the threequarter line. Because of their angles of support running, the back row should be close to any breakdown that results from a threequarter's solid defensive efforts.

Therefore one or more of the back-row players should always be close to the action and hopefully will be very quick to support any player tackling an opponent in possession to help to recover and secure the ball for his team.

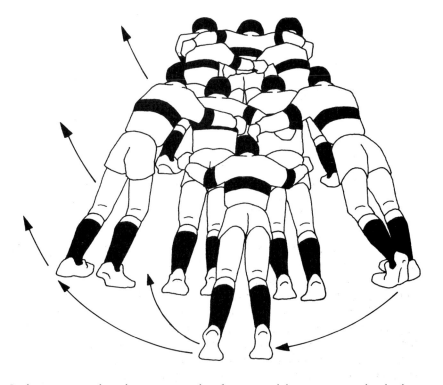

Back-row coverage from the scrummage: their first responsibilities are to cover breaks close to the set piece before advancing towards the fly-half and covering across the field supporting the threequarters, following the movement of the ball

To improve the defensive strategy of the team and the effectiveness of the back row, the threequarters should run to the outside shoulder of their opposite number, restricting the space for the outside break but encouraging an attempt at breaching their defensive formation on the inside. The attacking player should then be tackled by the covering back row, who will momentarily have a numerical advantage over their opponents to help to recover and secure the ball.

Although this can be an effective defensive strategy, there are occasions when the back row are unable to cover across the field to shepherd the opposing threequarters from the scrummages. Because their first responsibility concerns the defence close to the source of possession, the back-row players will sometimes be committed to tackle the breaking scrum-half and obviously incapable of covering across the field as quickly. Consequently the threequarters must obviously be aware of the limitations of the back-row cover under these circumstances and adapt accordingly.

The fly-half, appropriate flanker and number eight should perform their defensive duties from the scrummages as a co-ordinated unit attempting to prevent the opposing fly-half from distributing the ball to the threequarters. Although every player should always be responsible for countering the actions of his opposite number, it can prove worthwhile to stagger the arrival of this small defensive unit attempting to increase the pressure on the opposing fly-half. At the appropriate opportunity one of the defensive trio can overrun the fly-half receiving the ball, encouraging the inside break to be nullified by the other two advancing defenders.

Other features of forward tactical play

During the set pieces and transitional contests the most important criterion is that the forwards win and secure possession of the ball. Once this has been achieved, the players have the choice of two options:

1 releasing the ball quickly to the scrum-half, or
2 retaining possession to attack and attempt to drive forwards to cross the gain line.

With either option it is vital that the forwards commit all the opposing forwards in attempting to stop the progress of their drive. The opposing back-row forwards always prefer to hover on the fringes of the contests to attack the scrum-half's efforts and attempt to prevent possession from being distributed successfully to the threequarters. By winning the ball quickly and transferring it immediately to the scrum-half, the forwards can limit the effectiveness of the opposing back row. Also, the forwards and scrum-half an drive forwards close to the set pieces and commit the opposing back-row players to tackle the advancing ball carrier.

Kick-offs and drop-outs

Securing possession during the restarts can be achieved on a regular basis as a result of structured and repetitive practice. The most important factor during the restarts is the consistency of the player responsible for the kick-off in delivering the ball accurately to the target area. The flight of the ball should be high enough to provide the chasing forwards with sufficient time so that they arrive at the target area when the ball is in reach. To improve the concentration of the participants and to add realism for the players, the coach should introduce opponents to make the practice more competitive and realistic.

The forwards must master an effective routine to collect possession, and develop successful strategies to protect the catching player's efforts to secure the ball. Every forward player should be involved in the regular restart practices to become aware of his important role and familiar with his necessary contribution. It is important that the hooker is protected during the kick-offs and is given a covering defensive role during the execution of these set plays to prevent this important player from receiving an unfortunate injury during the combative restarts.

Receiving the kick-off or drop-out

When the ball is kicked high towards the touchline, the target players attempting to catch or deflect the ball towards a team-mate are the lock forwards. These players should position themselves close to the touchline and move forwards, attempting to catch or accurately deflect the ball at the highest possible point during its flight. It is vital that the players waiting to receive the ball quickly assess the flight and time their movement forwards so that they are not stationery when making contact with the ball. Once the ball has been caught or recovered, the other forwards should bind onto the player in possession to block the efforts of their opponents, secure the ball and drive forwards as a compact unit.

The coach must determine the individual role of each player during every conceivable eventuality and make players aware of the importance of their contribution. Below are a selection of some possible permutations and strategies for coaches to consider when preparing a team to receive the ball kicked in the conventional 22-metre drop-out and the traditional kick-off from the centre of the field.

Ploy 1 If number five catches the ball, number one blocks on the right-hand side, number four blocks on the left-hand side, while the number eight secures possession.

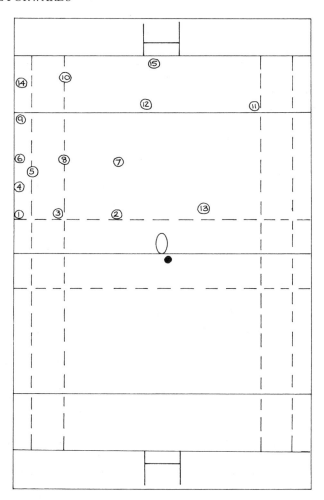

Receiving the kick-off: defensive starting positions to cover the high, lobbed kick towards the touchline, or the long, diagonal kick to the corner

Ploy 2 If number four catches the ball, number one blocks on the right-hand side, number three blocks on the left-hand side, while the number eight again secures possession.

Ploy 3 If numbers six or eight catch the ball, the player runs forwards and drives into the oncoming opponents, committing them to the tackle, and receives blocking support from the two closest team-mates, probably both prop forwards. Otherwise the player in possession can pass the ball immediately to the scrum-half to distribute to the threequarters or kick into touch to improve the territorial position.

Ploy 4 If the kick-off is poorly executed and the number seven catches the ball, he runs forwards to exploit the space and has the option of linking up with the other forwards to commit the chasing players, or distributing the ball to the supporting threequarters. They can then further expose the deficiencies in the defensive formation and continue the progress of the team by kicking for position or running and interpassing the ball.

Ploy 5 Occasionally a team will opt to kick the ball deep at the kick-off, attempting to immediately pressurise their opponents close to the latters' own goal line and the touchline, improve their field position and earn the throw-in to the line-out resulting from the receiving player kicking the ball into touch. Therefore the team need to ensure that their defensive formation adequately covers as much of the field as possible.

The half-backs should assume deep positions near the corner of the same side of the field as the opposing forwards who are preparing to follow the kick-off. The full-back should be positioned between the goal posts to counter the long kick-off straight down the field. Also, one of the centres and both wingers should be covering in deep positions and ready to support a counter-attack that either involves running the ball back towards their opponents or chasing a ball that has been kicked for touch.

Once the forwards have secured the ball and committed the opposing players to the ensuing ruck or maul, it is important that the team in possession attempt to drive their opponents backwards. The players should incorporate their rucking or mauling skills and continue to progress beyond the gain line to ensure that they commit all the opposing forwards standing around the fringes of the maul before distributing the ball to the scrum-half. By continuing to drive forwards, the players will create an attacking opportunity on the short side of the pitch for the number six, scrum-half and blind-side winger to exploit.

It is important that the scrum-half determines when the ball is released from the maul and is constantly encouraging and marshalling the efforts and movements of the forwards. The instructions and directions given by the scrum-half should ensure the continuity of play, helping the forwards to secure, retain and utilise the possession effectively.

Executing the kick-off or drop-out

The player taking the kick-off must be consistent in the execution of the skill, regularly delivering the ball into a predetermined and defined target area. The forwards should carefully assess the flight of the ball and advance towards the target area in groups. The first line of forwards should consist of the tallest players, including both the second-row players, sometimes supported by the number eight. The immediate objectives of these players are to try to catch the ball or deflect it downwards towards one of the second group of supporting players, consisting of the front row and flankers.

When players are unable to secure possession or reach the ball, they must attempt to prevent their opponents from driving the ball down the field. Carefully assessing the flight of the ball and determining the appropriate action to perform for the benefit of his team is obviously the responsibility of every forward. To jump and compete for the ball when there is little or no chance of affecting the outcome is both foolhardy and unnecessary. The efforts of the chasing players will prove much more productive and effective for their team if they restrain their competitive urge to commit themselves to an unsuccessful challenge for the ball. The most sensible option, which would prove much more appropriate and beneficial, would be to drive into the catching and protecting players to restrict their forward momentum and possibly cause a handling error that could result in a team-mate recovering possession.

A team unable to secure possession at the restarts of kick-off and drop-out must attempt to disrupt the quality of ball secured by their opponents and restrict the space available to limit the number of possible attacking options. The advancing flankers and hooker must delay their arrival at the point of collecting and protecting possession from the kick-off, and position themselves to defend around the fringes of the developing ruck or maul. It is important that these players are aware of their defensive responsibilities at the restarts and prevent opposing forwards from rolling and driving clear of the ruck or maul, as well as monitor the half-backs' efforts and attempt to restrict their productive contribution.

To improve their achievements at the restarts, a team can kick the ball deep towards their opponents' goal line but within the playing boundaries to force a defender to play the ball. Generally, threequarters prefer to run and pass the ball to their left, and the majority of players favour kicking the ball with their right foot. Therefore a team employing this tactical variation should kick the ball deep towards the junction of the left touchline and their opponents' goal line to effectively limit:

1 the amount of available space and attacking options that the player collecting possession has to run with the ball, and
2 successfully restrict the size of the angle and the time available for kicking the ball into touch to relieve the pressure and improve their team's field position.

This can be an effective ploy when executed correctly because the team responsible for the kick-off can considerably improve their field position and earn the throw-in to the resulting line-out.

Line-outs

Once the ball has crossed the touchline and the line-out is awarded, each team must include a minimum of two players and a maximum of all eight forwards in this restart of play. There are numerous options available to the team throwing the ball into the line-out, as they are able to dictate the length of the line-out, and their opponents must quickly react to the imposed tactical limitations.

The most important factor concerning the tactics at the line-out is the ability of the player to deliver the ball by throwing accurately between the two teams to the intended receiver. The second-row and number eight players are usually the tallest in each team and therefore also the intended targets for the thrower. Each specialist line-out jumper has normally practised individually with a coach to develop his own effective techniques and styles to successfully secure his own ball. The player throwing in to the line-out must practise with the receivers to master the required delivery that meets their particular criteria regarding the type and speed of service they require and be able to successfully flight the ball exactly when, where and how each of the players want it thrown.

The other forwards are required to compress the line-out to block the advances of the opposition and prevent them from reaching the ball to disrupt the quality of the possession. Two players are also required to sweep the line-outs to protect the scrum-half, securing and improving the quality of the possession caught and deflected by the second row or number eight. Because the starting positions of the specialist line-out jumpers can be varied, as well as the type and distance of the throw-in, it is necessary to nominate two different players to fulfil the duties of the sweeper, giving one of the front-row forwards the responsibility of covering the rear of the line-out and using one of the back-row players to sweep the front half.

The logic and reasoning behind this tactic is the fact that the scrum-half is one of the most valuable players and key decision makers in the team and should not have to deal with poor-quality possession. The forwards are the ball winners at the line-outs and their responsibilities are to win and secure good ball for the scrum-half; any poor possession should be retained and driven towards the opponents' goal line. Designating the role of sweeper to two particular players will simplify the responsibilities of the other forwards and ensure that their efforts are concentrated on compressing, blocking and driving the opposition backwards.

It is important that every player is familiar with the demands of his role at the line-outs, because the efforts and successes of the forwards in this set piece can help to dominate and control the developments in the match and consequently determine the outcome. There are usually more line-outs than any other set piece in a game of rugby football, which of course means that they are a very important source of possession. During the line-outs the team throwing in the ball have an obvious advantage, but it is not as beneficial or as productive as the feed into the scrummages. Both teams have a relatively equal chance of winning and securing possession from the line-outs; therefore each team should be well prepared and rehearsed in the techniques and requirements of specific defensive and attacking line-out ploys.

Communication

Good organisation at the line-outs requires the forwards to participate in regular repetitive practices to establish a variety of attacking ploys and determine the role of every player during this set piece. Communication at the line-out is a vital factor in ensuring a successful performance; every player must be conversant with the codes of signals that are given to designate the target area for a particular type of throw. The scrum-half is the best-placed player and most logical choice to communicate the signals to the forwards. There are many methods and codes of signals that can be devised to communicate the strategic intentions at the line-outs.

The most successful signals are ones that are the easiest to understand and remember: these may include verbal commands, physical gestures or a combination of the two. Although the signals need to be straightforward and easily recognisable for the unit of players responsible for the throw-in, they should be sufficiently obscure to prevent the opposing team from breaking the codes and deciphering the intentions. To benefit from the advantage of possession, it is important that the team responsible for the throw-in devise codes of signals that they can interchange to confuse their opponents.

Attempting to break and decipher the opponents' code of signals is usually the responsibility of the hooker or player marking the thrower-in. By careful observation of the scrum-half, monitoring of the signals and the resulting execution of the throw-in, it is possible to decipher the methods of communication. Breaking the opponents' means of communication can prove very useful to a team because they are then able to limit the advantage of possession, confidently and consistently competing against the intended receiver of the ball. The team are also able to implement strategies to directly contest for possession of the ball and organise their defences to counter any attacking ploys attempted by their opponents.

If a player has succeeded in breaking the code of signals used at the line-out, it is important to inform team-mates confidentially and quietly at the earliest opportunity rather than audibly announce the fact to the other forwards. This enables his team to exploit the decoder's cunning skills and provide a greater supply of possession for their threequarters to benefit from the extra space available at the line-outs.

Making use of possession

There are numerous strategies and options available for teams winning the ball at the line-out to make effective use of possession and vary the point of attack. The ball can be deflected or quickly transferred to the scrum-half for distribution to the threequarters, or the forwards can take the opportunity to implement a range of options. To pressurise opponents and commit their defensive cover to tackle the ball carrier close to the set piece, a team can:

1 withdraw one or more forwards from the line-out and distribute the ball to one of these players adopting the starting position of the fly-half, or
2 use a player to execute a peel around the front or back of the lines.

  Peeling from the line-out is an effective tactic because the ball carrier and supporting players are able to directly attack the weaker defensive areas of their opponents. The peel around the front involves one player from the back row receiving the ball from the front line-out specialist and driving upfield in between the touchline and the five-metre line. The peel around the back involves one of the front row forwards receiving the ball from the line-out specialist standing towards the rear of the line.

  The intentions of both peels are to commit the opposition players close to the set piece and attack the space around the line-outs to progress beyond the gain line. The peel around the front can be very effective because it can surprise the defending team and also extend the space available for the threequarters should the momentum of the forwards be halted and the ball be released to the half-backs. The intention of the front-row forward responsible for executing the peel around the back of the line is to run directly at the opposing fly-half, committing the player to performing a tackle.

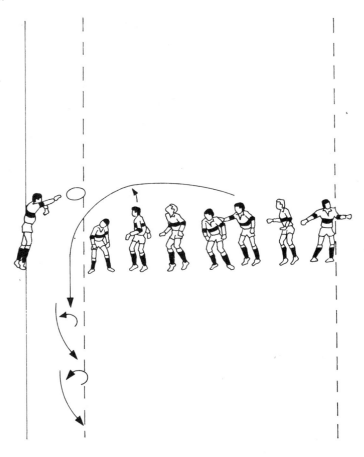

Peeling around the front of the line-out

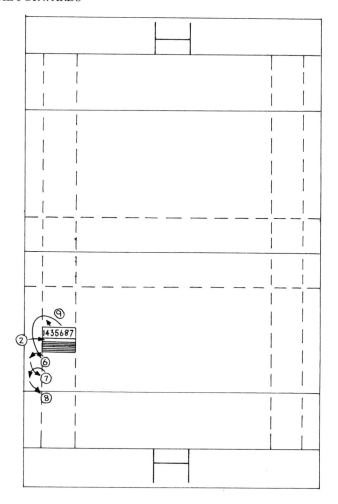

Peeling around the front of the line-out

It is the responsibility of the player in possession to make the ball available for the supporting forwards by one of the following means:

1 turning in the tackle to place the ball on the ground behind the contact point for the next player to decide whether to pick up the ball or create a ruck

2 turning the outside shoulder to the touchline on contact to protect possession before distributing the ball with a shield pass, or

3 driving in very low to an opponent and raising the upper body on contact with the defender remaining balanced on the feet to create a maul.

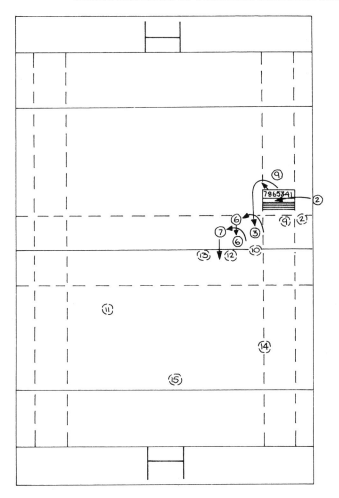

Peeling around the back of the line-out

The players need to practise these different techniques to decide on the most effective one for keeping the progress parallel to the touchline and the most successful one in maintaining control of the play to retain possession of the ball.

Securing possession

When a team are dominating and regularly securing good possession from the line-outs, they will be able to control a great deal of the play and frustrate their opponents' achievements. When a team are experiencing difficulty in securing their own ball in these set pieces, they should attempt to vary their tactics and upset their opponents' rhythm by altering the length of the line-outs and reducing the number of players directly involved.

Continually varying the number of participants in the line-out is as important as changing the length of the line. Sometimes a team sensibly reduce the number of players involved to the minimum of two forwards and successfully interrupt the concentration and rhythm of their opponents. However, they never take full advantage of the disruption, because the opposing team are usually prepared for the conventional reduction of the line-out to two players.

Confusion occurs when a team regularly vary:

1 the numbers of the participants
2 the length of the line, and
3 the distance between their players standing in the line-out, creating irregular gaps of more than the required distance of one metre.

The opposing forwards will be distracted as a result of the imposed changes and will begin to focus their attention on counting and reacting to the movement of players, rather than concentrating on their own performances in the line-out.

The team responsible for the throw-in can also determine the speed and continuity of the game. When the ball crosses the touchline to go out of play, the laws do not require the player recovering the ball to wait for the line-out to form before throwing the ball infield, unless a spectator or someone other than a player has touched the ball. Players can take advantage of their opponents arriving slowly at the line-out to throw the ball into play, providing the throw is straight and the ball travels the required five metres. Players can even throw the ball infield and then play the ball themselves to exploit the available time and space to secure and utilise possession.

There are numerous ploys and opportunities for a team to rehearse, practise and execute to ensure that they secure possession during the line-out contests. This particular restart of play requires players to adapt their individual skills, developing a cohesive and effective unit that is capable of winning the ball at the line-outs and can legally disrupt the efforts of their opponents. It is not often possible for the line-out specialists to catch the ball cleanly at these set pieces, although there are some exceptional exponents who on occasion are capable of securing such very good, controlled ball.

More often than not the ball is deflected by the target player with either one or two hands, attempting to guide the ball towards the scrum-half or directly to the support player standing immediately in front. Regular practice is essential to improve the accuracy of the deflection, co-ordinating the performance and developing the understanding of the supporting players to help to ensure the control of valuable possession.

Defending from the line-outs

The most obvious defensive strategy involves the line-out specialists directly competing against their opponents for the ball thrown into this particular set piece. By studying the various techniques of the thrower, the opposing players can note any particular mannerisms during the preparations or action when releasing the ball, to determine the intended destination point and target player for the throw. This observation, in conjunction with players attempting to break the code of signals that the opposition use to communicate to the intended receiver, will enable a team to limit their opponents' success during the line-outs, contributing to an effective defensive strategy.

To develop and extend this disruptive approach, a team can utilise one player positioned at the front of the line-out to raise both arms to create an awkward physical obstacle that their opponents must avoid when throwing the ball into the line-out. To further inconvenience their opponents, the defending team can move a tall player to the front of the line-out to fulfil the same role and also jump to contest for the ball once released by the thrower. These strategies can prove very effective because they can:

1 force the thrower to alter the flight and delivery of the ball
2 hinder the line-out specialist's view of the ball, and consequently
3 disrupt the timing of the line-out specialist jumping for the ball.

Other disruptive strategies at the line-outs involve players attempting to breach their opponents' defensive formation before they are capable of compressing the length of the line-out to consolidate and secure possession of the ball. The laws determine the spacing of individual participants within each team as well as the required distance that each respective line of players should be standing from their opponents. The spaces between each player in the line-out are potential gaps for opponents to penetrate and disrupt the scrum-half's efforts to distribute the ball successfully to the threequarters.

Good spacing at the line-out

Good compression of the line-out to protect and secure possession

Consequently the forwards must compress the length of the line-out as soon as the laws permit, to protect their scrum-half from the extra pressure imposed by opponents attempting to breach their line-out formation. All the players involved in the line-out should step towards the specialist jumper targeted for the intended reception of the ball, to close the gaps. While moving, the support players must be conscious of the flight of the ball and be ready to respond to any deflections to secure possession. Obviously closing the gaps is a necessity, but possession is the priority and players must react accordingly to collect the ball.

The technique of binding onto players to protect the line-out specialist, the ball and the scrum-half, is obviously important and should be practised

n training to determine the most appropriate and comfortable technique for
each player. A successful physical barrier to resist the challenges of
opponents will provide time for players to secure possession and ensure that
he scrum-half is also given the necessary time to accurately distribute the
ball to the threequarters.

The players either side of the specialist line-out exponent must create the
most secure and effective block, moving quickly into position to bind onto
the target player at the highest point of the jump when competing for the
ball. On returning to the ground, the ball should be protected from the
challenges of the opposing players, and both teams should attempt to drive
forwards to pressurise their opponents. It is important for the defending
team to attempt to initiate a forward drive in their efforts to recover the ball
or disrupt the quality of possession. The efforts of the team in possession
attempting to counter the effects of the drive could provide an opening for a
defending player to successfully reach over the blocking players to challenge
for the ball.

Players competing for the ball in a reduced line-out

The last player from each team in the line-out normally prefers to remain detached from the block to concentrate on pressurising and covering the half-backs, or tackling a player peeling around the back of the line-out. However, for the team losing possession every player should attempt to breach the physical barrier to spoil the quality of possession and prevent the transfer of the ball to the scrum-half. Preventing the opposition from distributing the ball away from the source of possession is much easier and more profitable than attempting to implement a defensive strategy to counter the movement of the ball and players in open space. Therefore both the last player in the line-out and the player involved in throwing in should also attempt to encroach around the front or back of the line-out to increase the pressure on the scrum-half receiving the ball, attempting to interfere or prevent the transfer of the ball to the fly-half.

Sweeping up poor-quality possession at the line-out

Once the ball is successfully transferred to the fly-half, the efforts of the last defensive player in the line-out should be to impose as much pressure as possible on the receiving player. All three back-row members and the fly-half should operate as a defensive unit, attempting to force the attacking outside half into the performance of an error, to restrict the effectiveness of the attacking team exploiting the use of possession. On occasion one of the players from this defensive unit should attempt to isolate the fly-half from the rest of the threequarters by deliberately but very slightly overrunning the player in possession, with the intention that the ball carrier should be either:

1 confused by the number of options available with the result that the execution of a passing ploy is cancelled, delayed and becomes less effective, or

2 encouraged to exploit the space close to the set piece and run into the advancing back-row players.

After pressurising the opposing fly-half, the back-row players perform the same covering duties, running across the field to reinforce the defensive formation of their threequarters. The half-backs should also cover the threequarters and back-row players to act as a third wave of defensive support to help out the full-back and respective winger.

Rucks and mauls

These are the transitional contests that provide the continuity of play and involve teams competing for second-phase possession when a ball carrier has been tackled or held by an opponent. The rucks and mauls occur only when possession has been secured during the first phase contests of the scrummages and line-outs. Although they are important features of rugby football and can provide an excellent supply of ball, they are of secondary importance to the set-piece restarts.

The objective of the ruck and maul is to recover, retain and secure possession, committing as many defenders as possible by driving forwards towards the opponents' goal line before releasing the ball to the scrum-half. Players involved in rucks and mauls should always be aware of these facts and be prepared to release the ball to the scrum-half at the earliest opportunity and not delay the continuity and flow of the game by extending the physical contest.

As well as occurring during open play and often referred to as the points of breakdown of a movement, the ruck and maul are sometimes utilised as a development of the restarts of the game, particularly the line-outs and kick-offs. The player securing possession under pressure requires immediate support from team mates to bind together and create a physical barrier of personnel to block, protect and secure the ball from their opponents. This co-ordinated movement should ensure the retention of the ball and create a solid platform to drive forwards and produce quality possession for the scrum-half to exploit the situation or distribute to the threequarters.

The effectiveness of a team rucking or mauling the ball is determined by their level of success at securing and retaining possession of it. Both these phases of play are established when a defender tackles the ball carrier; players must ruck with their feet when the ball is released or placed on the ground to fulfil the requirements of the laws of the game. Teams are able to maul the ball and transfer it through their hands when the players in possession are able to thwart the defenders' efforts and stay on their feet, creating a target for the support players to establish a driving spearhead.

Players caught in possession in an isolated defensive position with few immediate support players and outnumbered by their opponents should be capable of successfully mauling the ball to limit the other team's advantage. It is vital under these circumstances that the ball carrier does not go to ground and be forced to release the ball immediately for the opposing players to recover possession. The tactical ploy should be to delay the release of the ball for as long as possible while conforming to the laws of the game and standing to contest the efforts of the opponents. This will provide a target and extend the time for the support players to arrive at the breakdown point, effectively helping to retain and protect vital possession of the ball.

Players arriving at the breakdown should make sure that they enter the ruck or maul at the most effective point to contribute to the drive and maintain the security of the ball.

The ruck

The traditional rucking technique requires the player tackled in possession to place the ball on the ground under control, falling with his body between his opponents and the ball, establishing a physical barrier to briefly shield the position of the ball. The first support players to arrive at the point of the breakdown then drive over the player on the ground, binding together and making contact with members of the opposing team to create a platform for the arrival of the following support players. All the arriving reinforcements then bind onto their team-mates and drive forwards, stepping over the ball to leave it for the scrum-half.

As well as this classic rucking method, recent developments in the modern game have resulted in the creation of two other rucking techniques. The post ruck involves the ball carrier driving low into the defender and releasing the ball through the legs at the moment of contact. It is necessary that the player releasing the ball has players in close support but in positions where it is impossible to securely transfer the ball to them. Once the ball is placed on the ground the original attacking player must continue to drive the defender backwards and create a target for the support players to bind onto and add their weight and power to continue the forward momentum.

The sink ruck is a development of a maul, when the player in possession has difficulty in successfully transferring the ball to a support player because of the actions of the tackling player and the defenders preventing the ball from being released. Under these circumstances the player in possession must lower his centre of gravity and body weight to force himself to drop to the ground with the ball, freeing himself from the attentions of his opponents and securing the retention of possession. Once the player falls to the ground, the ball is released and the remainder of the forwards drive over the ball or channel it back to the scrum-half.

The maul

The maul has also been developed in the modern game to exert pressure on opponents by attempting to keep them moving backwards. Everyone involved in the maul should be made aware of the position of the ball as the players communicate with one another. The driving and rolling mauls are variations of improving the continuity of the game and ensuring the supply of good second-phase possession, with the team harnessing the players' power and ball-smuggling skills to keep the mauls moving forwards and the team progressing towards the opponents' goal line.

The French forwards have secured possession in the maul and are trying to advance towards their opponents' goal line before releasing the ball to the scrum-half

The rolling maul is effective in continuing the forward momentum by altering the spearhead of the drive and committing the defending players hovering on the fringes of the breakdown into performing tackles. To initiate a rolling maul, one of the support players must take the ball from the ball carrier with one hand while at the same time pulling that player around to alter the point of attack. The movement continues with each subsequent ball carrier turning his back on the opponents to create a physical barrier to

Solid platform for the maul

protect the ball and help to pull the next available support player around to the side of the maul to ensure the safe transfer of possession while the forward momentum is maintained. By altering the spearhead of the drive close to the sides of the maul, the fringing players are involved and committed in their efforts to prevent the advance of the player in possession. Once all the fringing players and first line of defence are involved in the maul, the next rolling player should be able to progress upfield by attacking the space created close to the sides of the maul.

Once the forward momentum of the driving maul is countered by their opponents, some teams begin to implement a continuous rolling maul and constantly alter the spearhead of the attack. Providing the players are able to continue their forward progress, this can be a worthwhile option, but only if their efforts succeed in committing the fringing defenders into the maul and if a player in possession is regularly released to attack the threequarters with good, close support from the other forwards.

A subtle and successful development of the maul is for the players to concentrate their drive through the centre of the contest. Rather than alter the spearhead of the drive by rolling around to the outsides of the maul, this method concentrates the drive through the centre of the maul, which is often the weakest defensive point. The effects are the same in that the team in possession should succeed in their efforts to continue the forward momentum and commit the fringing players into the maul in their attempt to counter the forward progress of the team in possession. However, the advantages are that the ball carrier will have gained more ground in a shorter time and there will be players in close support available on both sides.

Initiating this development requires the support players to secure the ball by binding and driving the player caught in possession to prevent their opponents from handling the ball. Rather than forming a wide defensive block, the support players bind tightly together and concentrate their efforts on recreating a scrummaging formation. When all the players are involved in the maul, the ball carrier transfers possession to the nearest support player, slightly altering the spearhead of the attack. This subtle change of emphasis can expose the other team's defensive deficiencies in the centre of the maul and result in the player in possession being driven clear by the co-ordinated

Securing and protecting possession at the maul

The ball is well protected by the player's body, to allow the support players to drive over to maintain forward momentum at the ruck

efforts of his team-mates. Each ball carrier in turn can help to maintain the forward drive by continuously communicating with the support players, by performing rolling movements to change the emphasis of the attack, and by using his body weight to exploit a defensive weakness.

4 Penalty ploys

Attacking with penalty kicks

Infringements of the laws of the game and playing indiscretions result in penalty kicks being awarded against the guilty team by the referee. These can provide a range of several attacking opportunities for the team receiving possession of the ball. In competitive games there are numerous occasions when the participants commit offences that contravene the laws. It is the response of the referee and other players that can determine the consequences of these actions and whether or not it is beneficial to the innocent team for the referee to award a penalty. Often this team are able to exploit an advantage when the referee allows play to continue and therefore all players should respond only to the referee's whistle, and should continue playing until they hear it.

A team can exploit the benefit of a penalty award in one of the following ways.

a Depending on the penalty award the captain opts for a place kick or drop kick at goal in an attempt to score three points for the team.
b Kicking for touch or diagonally across the field improves the territorial position or takes advantage of the poor defensive formation, to attack the space and pressurise the opposition.
c The ball can be kicked high and sufficiently forwards for the chasing players to arrive at the point where the ball is falling into a playable position, pressurising the waiting defensive opponents; this type of kick is often referred to as an 'up and under' or 'Garryowen'.
d The short, tapped kick of the ball through the mark of the penalty gives players the chance to run at their opponents in an attempt to gain a numerical or territorial advantage and hopefully score a try.

The captain should quickly assess the field position, the deployment of all the players and the state of the game to decide upon the most appropriate option. Scoring three points from a penalty kick at goal and improving the field position are obviously important to maintain the pressure on opponents, but sometimes it is necessary to keep the ball in play and attempt to score a try to earn four points with the possibility of a further two points for the conversion. Therefore a team should practise developing a repertoire

Paul Thorburn (Wales) has regularly demonstrated the considerable benefit, importance and value of having a consistently successful goal kicker in the team

of short penalty movements that they are capable of executing successfully from various positions around the field.

The first option that the captain and key decision makers should consider when their team have been awarded a penalty is the possible success of a goal kick. Important points are earned from converting penalty awards into three points for the team with a place kick or drop kick at goal. The value of a reliable, accurate and efficient place kicker and drop-kick expert cannot be stressed enough, because their contribution to the team performance can prove to be the difference between success and failure, between winning or losing a competitive game. The ability of the attacking team to consistently convert penalty awards into points also has a very positive effect on team spirit and morale. Conversely, opposing players can become frustrated, which has a negative effect on their performance, disrupting team harmony and unity. Players appreciate their efforts being rewarded, and scoring three points from a penalty kick helps everyone to sustain their contribution to maintain pressure on their opponents.

The second option very much depends on the field position and the state of the game, as mentioned earlier. The captain must decide the most effective action, whether to kick the ball to improve the territorial position, to exploit a weakness in the defensive formation, or to pressurise a particular individual player, for example the full-back.

The short, tapped penalty

When kicking the ball is not considered the most effective option, the next consideration should be electing to execute a short, tapped penalty ploy. The intention of this is to run the ball at the opposition to score a try or commit the defensive players to a ruck or maul situation to improve the amount of space available in other areas of the field.

Each tapped penalty ploy should have been carefully rehearsed in training to ensure that every player is familiar with his contribution in the overall performance of the movement. Before nominating a particular set ploy from the repertoire, it is vital that the captain assesses the opponents' defensive formation to identify any weaknesses and to help to select the most relevant movement to exploit the advantage of possession. When opponents are prepared to defend a tapped penalty the captain must elect the most suitable ploy that will eventually result in a scoring opportunity. The penalty ploys should contribute to the agreed game plan to attack the narrow side of the field, the central area or wide out.

The most important criteria concerning the successful execution of short, tapped penalty ploys include:

1 the speed of the captain to make a decision and communicate the intentions to the remainder of the team

2 the reaction of the players to respond to the signal and assume their correct start and support positions

3 the speed of the player responsible for the execution of the tapped penalty to move to the mark made by the referee designating the place of the award

4 the speed of transferring the ball to the player responsible for executing the tapped penalty, and

5 the deployment, defensive formation and state of readiness of the players from both teams.

Below are a selection of short penalty ploys that a team can rehearse and perfect during training sessions for their successful execution during a game situation. Some penalty ploys involve speed of movement to surprise or deceive opponents, while others require players to run on different timing patterns and in varied directional sequences.

Using speed of movement

Ploy 1 The leader of the forwards recovers the ball to take a short, tapped penalty through the mark and drives towards the nearest opponent to commit that defensive player before passing the ball to a close-running support player who continues the progress of the movement. It is important that all the forwards are prepared as a unit for this ploy and react quickly to run into close-support positions as soon as the penalty is awarded by the referee. The intention is to continue the flow of play without delay to prevent the opposing team from regrouping their personnel or reorganising their defensive formation to cover the depleted areas of the field and stifle any attacking opportunities.

To prove successful and effective in retaining and utilising possession from the resulting transitional phase of play, the forwards must be realistic in their efforts and control their enthusiasm to progress too far downfield when in possession. The distribution of the ball to the scrum-half from the resulting ruck or maul must be quick, to exploit the confusion and available spaces in the defensive formation of their opponents.

A variation on this ploy is for the scrum-half to recover possession to perform the short, tapped penalty before transferring the ball with a short pass to a forward running at speed and supported on either side and by players in depth to create an attacking spearhead formation.

Ploys that concentrate on the quick movement of the ball to maintain the continuity of play revolve around the attacking team's ability to expose their opponents' defensive inadequacies by the speed of their actions. Because of superior organisation, the attacking team can often afford to plan to withdraw a forward from the initial performance of the short, tapped penalty. This player can be successfully utilised to further penetrate the opponents' defensive formation by receiving the pass from the scrum-half distributing possession retained from the resulting ruck or maul.

Ploy 2 The scrum-half takes the tapped penalty and distributes the ball to the fly-half, who does one of the following things.

a He makes a simple and straightforward passing movement to transfer the ball quickly to the winger to attack the space on the flanks.
b He performs a predetermined passing ploy among the threequarters to deceive the opposition that the ball is going to be transferred to the winger, before executing a switch pass with one of the centres or a good ball-handling forward positioned slightly behind the threequarters. The player in possession runs back towards the team's remaining forward unit and commits an opponent to the tackle, before transferring the ball to a support player to hopefully exploit a numerical advantage over the defensive cover.
c He transfers the ball with a short pass to one of the back-row forwards running straight to attack the space between the opposing fly-half and inside centre.

Obviously the most important criterion determining the success of these ploys is an early signal announcing their selection and good communication between the players to prepare everyone for their execution.

Ploy 3 When a penalty is awarded within a few metres of the opponents' goal line, the scrum-half can position the ball on the mark and stand between the ball and the goal line, facing the forwards spread out in one line about ten metres away. On a pre-arranged signal, all the forwards run straight towards the goal line and the scrum-half takes the tapped penalty and passes the ball to a predetermined player. The advantages of this ploy include the ability of the advancing players to establish forward momentum compared with the restricted and stationery positions of the defending team. The difficulties for the defending team involve assessing the intended receiver of the ball and performing suitably successful strategies for halting the progress of the attacking team to prevent the ball carrier or subsequent support player from crossing the line to score a try.

A variation on this ploy involves the players assuming the same start positions and performing the same actions, except that the scrum-half kicks the ball over one shoulder and high over the goal line rather than passing it to an advancing forward. The defending team are usually expecting a forward to receive the ball and are eager to advance as soon as the tapped penalty has been taken to tackle the ball carrier in front of their goal line, leaving large areas of their in-goal area exposed for the attacking team to exploit.

Using a post player

The following ploys involve the use of a post player, which is the name given to the first receiver of the pass standing about eight metres away from and almost level with the scrum-half taking the tapped penalty. This player is often referred to as a pivot because of the demands of executing a central distributing role in the ploys. To contribute to the deception of the ploy, the post player or group of players stand with their backs to the opponents to shield the ball when in possession, making it difficult for the defending team to identify the eventual receiver of the short pass.

Ploy 1 The pivot player is used as a decoy to attract the defending team's attention but missed out with the pass as the ball is transferred directly to the fly-half. Once in possession, the fly-half can distribute the ball to the centre, a forward either running onto a short pass on the outside or altering the point of attack by passing the ball back inside to immediately link up with the remainder of the supporting forward unit.

A variation of this ploy in positioning the post as a decoy is to attempt to convince the opposition that the ball is once again to be distributed wide to the fly-half. Instead of executing a miss move, the ball is transferred with a short pass to one of the forwards running between the scrum-half and the post player to attack the space close to the mark of the penalty and hopefully exploit poor defensive coverage in that area.

Ploy 2 The ball is transferred to the post player and the scrum-half loops around to receive a return pass and do one of the following:

1 straighten the angle of running to attack and exploit any space between the opposing threequarters
2 continue running across the field and perform dummy scissors and switch passes with the threequarters and/or forwards positioned slightly behind the threequarters but who reveal themselves running straight and receive the ball from the scrum-half to penetrate their opponents' defensive formation or act as a decoy to distract attention from the intended receiver, or
3 distribute the ball immediately to the fly-half to execute a predetermined passing ploy among the threequarters with the support of the forwards.

Ploy 3 The ball is again transferred to the post player and the scrum-half loops around but does not receive a return pass, although the post player offers a dummy pass and the scrum-half pretends to receive possession. Hopefully the attentions of the defensive team will be distracted momentarily for the pivot player to turn towards the touchline to attack the space on the narrow side of the field. A simple development of this ploy would involve another forward running across the pivot player towards the narrow side of the field, to receive the ball and exploit the confusion to hopefully progress beyond the gain line.

This ploy can be further developed and extended to vary the point of the attack. It is important that each player performs the same function, and the ball is offered but retained by the post player. As soon as the scrum-half loops around the post player, a forward runs in the opposite direction owards the narrow side of the field, with a second forward immediately running across and behind the pivot player to the open side. The post player must offer the ball to each of the first two decoy runners by executing exaggerated dummy passes, before distributing possession to the third participant attacking the open-side spaces.

The vital components of the variations of this ploy are sound communication, understanding, good timing and good angles of approach running to receive the ball from the post player. The actions of each player involved in the ploy should momentarily distract the defenders and disguise the intended point of the attack, to enable the ball carrier to exploit any hesitation and progress beyond the gain line before being confronted and tackled by an opponent to establish a ruck or maul situation.

Ploy 4 The attacking team increase the number of players adopting the post position to extend the size of the physical barrier and thereby disguise the ball's position. The number of players involved in the formation of a screen of multi-pivots depends on the attacking team's intentions and can range from two to four players. To increase the number of options available from this extended post formation, each of the participants in the multi-pivot position should be slightly behind the player nearest the ball. They will then conform with the laws of the game should the ball be interpassed between these players, and should stand either:

1 shoulder to shoulder to form a complete physical barrier to shield the ball, or
2 with a variety of distances between each participant: in pairs with a gap between each group, with a small gap between all participants, or with irregular gaps between the players.

The greater the variety of starting positions of the multi-pivot players at the short, tapped penalty, the greater the pressure and difficulties for the opposing team attempting to organise a suitable defensive formation to counter the attacking team's actions. It is important that the attacking team maintain and exploit their advantage of the penalty award, causing as much confusion, distraction and concern among the defending team as possible. Involving more than four players in the multi-pivot could prove counter-productive because the number of options available to exploit this short, tapped penalty would be limited.

Using a multi-pivot
The same ploys as described above could also be performed with a multi-pivot, with the advantage that all the players involved in the post position would arrive at the breakdown point as one unit to add greater impetus to the drive at the ruck or maul situation. However, there are also a number of variations that can extend and subtly develop the repertoire of short, tapped penalty ploys using this multi-pivot formation.

Ploy 1 Two players stand in the post position with eight metres separating them from each other and the scrum-half. The intention of the second post player is to provide an extra option for the attacking team to transfer the ball to a position further away from the mark of the penalty award. Either one or both players can be involved in the execution of the tapped penalty, or can be positioned simply as a decoy to distract their opponents. Any of the ploys previously described can be executed using the first or second post player however, if the furthest participant is to assume the pivotal role, the ball must be transferred directly from the scrum-half for the movement to be effective.

Ploy 2 All the participants stand very close together in the post position before the ball is passed to the player nearest the scrum-half and transferred along the line of players, with the defending team unable to determine its actual position or intended destination. All the players break from the post position, pretending to carry the ball and running to attack predetermined areas of the field, one to the narrow side, one to the open side, one turning and running straight towards the opponents' goal line. When a fourth player is included in the multi-pivot position, this player can run in immediate close support of the ball carrier. The remainder of the attacking forwards are aware of the identity of the ball carrier and also run to support that player to produce a numerical advantage at the eventual breakdown point.

The intention of this ploy is to create as much movement away from the multi-post position as possible, with players running in different directions as decoys contributing to the deception. Hopefully the successful execution of the ploy will momentarily confuse the opposition and encourage them to break their covering formation unnecessarily to create gaps for the attacking players to exploit.

Ploy 3 The four post players again stand shoulder to shoulder to shield the ball transferred from the scrum-half, who immediately loops around, pretending to receive possession. During this decoy the ball is transferred to one of the central players, who turns to form a spearhead attack with the close support of the other participants. Running parallel to the touchline the players attempt to progress downfield, driving the player in possession of the ball.

Ploy 4 The participants in the post position again stand close together in a group of four to receive the ball from the scrum-half. The players break in pairs, with each turning predictably and slowly in opposite directions to create a gap between them to reveal a forward running at pace from a previously hidden and deep starting position directly behind the multi-pivot barrier. The approaching forward collects the ball from the nearest player turning towards the narrow side of the field, and continues through the gap to attack the space immediately in front of the dividing post position.

Ploy 5 The participants in the post position vary the distances that each player is standing from the other. The scrum-half passes the ball to one of the players furthest away, who waits for the other members of the multi-pivotal position to loop around and take the ball. The ball carrier drives towards an opposing player and performs the same actions as described in the peel round the back of the line-out, transferring the ball to the support player with a screen pass to continue the forward momentum towards the opponents' goal line.

Ploy 6 The participants in the multi-post position stand in pairs with a gap of two metres separating them. The ball is passed by the scrum-half to the nearest player who does one of the following things.

- He transfers possession to a forward running at pace through the gap.
- He gives a short pass to the next pair before both players loop around to allow one to receive the ball and drive forwards.
- He rolls off to the narrow side of the field to attack the space in front of the scrum-half, before performing a scissors with that player to change the direction of play. The scrum-half can immediately link up with the two support players who were standing as the furthest pair in the multi-post position.

All the above ploys are variations on attacking principles to create improved attacking positions, enabling a team to progress beyond the gain line and exploit the available space in the defensive formation. There are numerous alternatives for a team to perform to exploit good field positions and attacking opportunities when penalties are awarded by the referee. Every team should develop a good, varied repertoire of short, tapped penalty ploys that they can consistently perform to a high standard to complement their agreed game plan or vary the point of attack from these features of play. Coaches should provide opportunities for players to contribute their ideas, to describe and demonstrate the potential of a short, tapped penalty ploy that could prove a useful, effective and unique addition to the team's repertoire.

Defending against penalty kicks

Infringing the laws

Players guilty of infringing the laws of the game are penalised by the referee and immediately sacrifice the advantage of uncontested possession to their

opponents. The team awarded a penalty are able to control the use of th
ball, altering the flow of play, changing the course of the game and the fiel
position by exploiting the opportunities presented by a playing indiscretior
Because of these consequences coaches should regularly discuss th
importance and relevance of the laws of the game to make sure that player
are familiar with them. Every player should possess a working knowledg
and understanding of the laws for every playing situation that he is likely t
encounter during his participation in competitive fixtures.

Stressing during training sessions the need to adhere to the laws of th
game should help to encourage players to perform within them an
discourage them from infringing and disrupting the organisation an
success of the practice. However, there are occasions when the coach shoul
discuss with the players the situations during a game when they may have t
carefully consider the ramifications of committing a deliberate infringemen
of the laws for their team's benefit.

For example, an isolated defender gathering possession while coverin
across the field is unable to kick the ball safely into touch because of the clos
attention of several opponents. Being caught in possession in such
position, the ball carrier must compete against the efforts of the tacklers t
stay upright and thereby create a target for the recovering support player
However, should the ball carrier be overwhelmed by opponents and unab
to resist their challenges, resulting in the player being forced to the groun
the laws require the ball to be released immediately. At this point the playe
must make a very quick but possibly a vitally important decision based o
the consequences of such an action. If the defender decides that a try woul
probably be scored, improving the opposition's score by six points an
establishing an important psychological advantage, it may be prudent for th
ball carrier to delay the release of the ball and commit a deliberat
infringement of the laws. This is not in the spirit of the game, but the player'
actions could reduce the number of points scored by the opposing team t
only three resulting from the conversion of the penalty award. Many peop
would therefore argue that limiting the scoring success justified the player'
actions.

Players deserve to be punished for infringing the laws and therefor
everyone must carefully consider his actions when participating in trainin
to perform within the laws and learn to contribute within the recognised an
accepted framework of the game. Coaches are responsible for helpin
players to improve their technical performance as well as increasing thei
familiarity, awareness and understanding to become conversant with th
laws of the game.

Adopting the defensive position

Educating players to avoid penalties being awarded against them i
obviously the best form of defence. However, as mentioned above there ar

occasions when players decide to risk being penalised, infringing the laws in an attempt to limit the extent of the success of their opponents. When a penalty is awarded against a team-mate, every player must maintain his concentration, quickly retiring ten metres to comply with the laws, and position himself to cover any noticeable spaces or outstanding gaps in the defensive formation.

It is imperative that players do not turn their backs on their opponents when adopting their defensive position. Knowing the whereabouts of the ball at all times is very important, and running backwards into position will allow every player to keep watching the ball and be capable of responding quickly to the actions of his opponents by continually assessing the current state of play. The retiring team should communicate with one another, encouraging players to move into particular positions to cover possible defensive weaknesses in their formation. Responding quickly to other players' requests limits the options available for the team in possession, and that should be the priority of every defender.

On occasion, players are unaware of the reason for the penalty award against them and can be frustrated by the referee's decision. When this happens, it is the responsibility of the captain to politely request clarification from the referee to explain the infringement leading to the penalty award. During this enquiry the player or players responsible for committing the offence should immediately retire the obligatory ten metres to disassociate themselves from the discussion and concentrate on improving their team's defensive coverage of the field. The referee's response will always be concise, to allow play to continue without further delay to prevent the team awarded the penalty from losing the initiative, and the captain should inform the culprit at the most convenient and appropriate moment to discourage a repeat performance.

The defending team should initially organise their defensive formation to counter their opponents executing a short, tapped penalty to run with the ball, regardless of the field position. Adopting this strategy could possibly grasp the initiative from the attacking team, causing them to delay their intentions, further assess the situation and perhaps rethink their response. Organising a good defensive formation to counter a short, tapped penalty ploy requires teams to regularly rehearse their actions from every game situation to form an effective blanket coverage of the immediate area opposite and adjacent to the mark of the penalty award.

Defensive areas and zones

It is valuable for the coach and players to spend time during training highlighting the most vulnerable defensive areas and zones, prioritising and designating the ones that need to be covered by the retiring defenders. The preparation and state of readiness of the defending team can cause opponents to delay the execution of their penalty award or decide to change their original intention. The resulting delay in taking the penalty can prove beneficial to the defending team, allowing players to improve and alter their formation to adopt an even more effective defensive cover to counter the intentions of the team in possession.

When a penalty is awarded against a team, players should immediately retire to their defensive positions covering an area or zone predetermined by the coach and agreed upon during training. Players should fulfil their defensive responsibilities by holding their covering positions until either their opponents instruct the referee that they intend to kick for goal or they take the short, tapped penalty.

If the opposition decide to respond by executing a different ploy, for example kicking the ball to improve their field position, their intentions should become obvious from their actions and positioning of players. When it is apparent that the team in possession are clearly intent on kicking the ball upfield, one or both of the half-backs plus a back-row player should drop further downfield towards their own goal line to improve the defensive cover supporting the full-back. The spaces left by the altered deployment of these players must be covered by defenders close to the mark of the penalty award, preventing the attacking team from quickly exploiting the newly created gaps by executing a short, tapped penalty.

Securing possession

The defensive formation to cover kicks upfield or goal attempts involves players moving into predetermined positions to exploit the use of possession should the execution of the kick be poor. The defending team must be prepared to cover and exploit all eventualities: for example, the ball rebounding from the crossbar or one of the posts when opponents have attempted to convert the penalty award into three points with a kick at goal. Should the ball strike the woodwork of the goal posts and rebound, the defending team must have players in numerous covering positions surrounding the target area, designated with the responsibility of recovering the ball deflected from the posts or crossbar.

Depending on the circumstances and the amount of pressure exerted by the players following the attempted kick at goal, the player recovering possession will be confronted with the following options:

1 allowing the ball to cross the goal line before collecting possession to touch down and stop the game, restarting play with a 22-metre drop-out
2 kicking the ball into touch to relieve the pressure and improve the field position, or
3 running with the ball to exploit the space and numerical advantage over his team's opponents.

Players prepared to delay securing possession to wait for the ball to travel across the goal line must be very careful that they have not miscalculated the

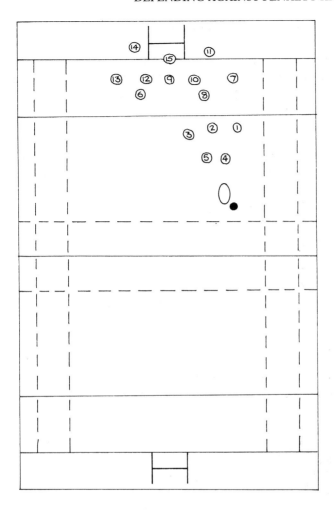

Covering positions to cover rebounds from the posts or crossbar from an attempted penalty kick by the opposition

situation and imposed unnecessary pressure on themselves or their team as a result. The shape of the rugby ball makes its actions unpredictable, and players anticipating certain developments can be both disappointed and embarrassed by the unexpected and sometimes freakish movement of the ball bouncing along the ground. Therefore players are well advised to choose the safest option when defending, catching the ball at the earliest opportunity and executing whatever option they perceive as the most effective for their team to relieve the pressure or build an attacking movement.

Limiting space

Coaches must focus players' attention and highlight the necessity of limiting the available space to restrict the number of attacking options open to their opponents. When opponents execute a short, tapped penalty ploy, there are several different defensive strategies that a team can employ to limit the effectiveness of the penalty.

Strategy 1 The players hold their starting positions to maintain their blanket-coverage formation, waiting for the sequences of movement and timing patterns of individual playing assignments of the ploy to unravel. Once the identity of the ball carrier and the target area for the attack are revealed, the defenders can perform tackles to restrict the ploy's success.

Strategy 2 All players in the blanket coverage advance together in their defensive formation to pressurise the team in possession, limiting the amount of time and space available for the execution and completion of the ploy.

Strategy 3 One defender is designated to quickly advance to threaten and hopefully tackle the post player in possession, or successfully impose sufficient pressure to disrupt the execution and effectiveness of the ploy. The remainder of the team either retain their starting positions or advance slowly as a defensive unit to limit the time and space available.

Every player has a significant function and responsibility in contributing towards the effectiveness of his team's defensive strategy. Every defender is important in, firstly, covering a specific area of the field and, secondly, maintaining a good, balanced body position to perform an effective tackle to successfully halt the progress of an opposing player running in possession of the ball. The defending team should always be prepared to exploit every situation to benefit from their ball-handling, elusive-running skills and accurate kicking expertise when the opportunities present themselves. Although attack can often prove the most successful form of defence, damage limitation is also an important factor when a team are recovering possession from their opponents executing a poor attacking ploy, whether an unsuccessful kick at goal or whatever.

It is a valuable and useful organisational exercise to concentrate players' attention on the consequences of their decisions and resulting actions. All players should be familiar with the overall game plan, the application of selected tactical ploys to achieve realistic objectives, and the importance of sound strategic planning. Highlighting the various outcomes and discussing possible alternatives proves more relevant and realistic when the playing area is considered as three separate sections: the attacking third, the middle third and the defensive third.

One of the most important factors contributing to a successful defensive strategy involves players maintaining their concentration rather than being sidetracked and venting their frustration, seeking to apportion blame for the award of a penalty to their opponents. Players must learn to control their emotions and channel their nervous energies into a positive contribution for their team rather than remonstrating with colleagues. Negative comments only succeed in causing unnecessary distractions, disrupting the attention and concentration of players on the immediate proceedings, and proving to be a negative influence on playing performances and team harmony.

Finding the most suitable solutions to effectively solve the problems set by the coach when specific game-related practices are organised in each particular area of the field can significantly contribute to a marked improvement in tactical awareness, application and understanding. Every training session should involve a period of time when the players work together as a team in structured practice situations, in which the emphasis is placed on the selection and execution of the most suitable and effective attacking and defending strategies to perform for the team's benefit.

5 Seven-a-side rugby

The basic principles of sevens

Sevens is an exciting and extremely entertaining derivative of rugby football, usually played in tournaments organised before and after the regular 15-a-side season. The game is peculiar in that the reduced numbers of players participating in sevens compete on a full-size pitch, increasing the amount of space available to cover and exploit. This provides numerous opportunities for players to demonstrate their skills, creating a special, relaxed, good-humoured and convivial atmosphere of excitement and anticipation for everyone involved.

All the players participating and competing in sevens tournaments need to be extremely fit and accomplished performers, proficient in the execution of all the basic skills of the game, particularly handling, balanced and elusive running, tackling, and securing possession. Because of the immense size of the pitch and the reduced numbers of players, there is a great deal of space available when playing sevens. As a result every player is continually tested by his opponents and regularly required to demonstrate his commitment and technical expertise.

Games are normally an explosive spectacle, condensing all the features of open rugby into two concentrated periods of seven or ten minutes' duration. The fundamental principles of playing seven-a-side are different to 15-a-side rugby because the most important factor in sevens is that the players win, secure and retain possession of the ball, regardless of the circumstances and field position.

Sevens rugby is a classic example of the vital importance of possession, giving the players a tremendous psychological advantage when they control the movement of the ball and the flow of play. Conversely, players unable to secure possession and required to defend for long periods of the game become frustrated, dejected and disheartened. Therefore keeping the ball is more important than attempting to progress towards the opponents' goal line. When a team have the ball they can determine the tactics and pace of the game, slowing proceedings to a standstill at times, scheming to create a numerical advantage and an attacking opportunity to outwit the defensive cover of their opponents.

During their participation in seven-a-side games, players should always be prepared to retreat to ensure they retain possession. Sometimes a team is involved in passing the ball around behind their own goal line, attempting to create a clear opportunity for one player to breach the opponents' defensive formation. The player in possession of the ball must always make sure that he is never isolated from his team-mates or outnumbered by the defending players.

It is important that the ball carrier carefully assesses the position and number of the defenders compared to the position of the nearest support player in a designated area, and considers the potential success rate of a direct attack against the possible risk of losing possession. This does not mean that the ball carrier should not attack an opponent when the opportunity arises; the onus is on the other players to move quickly into a support position to receive a pass or secure possession, should the attempt to breach the defensive formation fail.

When the attacking player is pressurised by one or more opponents, the ball must be passed away from the point of potential danger where possession is threatened. Ideally, the ball should be passed or released to a support player before the player in possession is tackled. However, on occasion this is not possible, and therefore every player must be practised and competent in performing the techniques of mauling and rucking to retain and secure possession.

Players should carry the ball in two hands as often as possible, to keep their options open and the ball readily available, enabling them to transfer the ball quickly and accurately. At times it will be necessary for players to hold the ball under the arm further away from the defender, to free the other hand to push away and resist the challenges of the tackler. Consequently players need to be capable of transferring the ball quickly, accurately and confidently to retain possession when under pressure.

The players

For many players, seven-a-side rugby is a great challenge and provides an excellent opportunity for them to demonstrate their individual skills, expertise, positional awareness, tactical acumen and enterprise. Every position demands the performance of specific techniques and each player has a particular role in contributing to the team effort.

Every player selected to play in the seven must be very comfortable in possession and have excellent handling skills to safely catch and successfully transfer the ball. Because of the pressure inflicted by the opposition, players must be able to adapt their technical expertise to each situation, competently and successfully demonstrating their skills in catching and passing the ball at different running speeds and over a range of distances.

Situations often arise in which the ball carrier must transfer the ball very quickly and improvise the execution of a pass to ensure continuity of play.

It is important that all the participating players are able to quickly assess the available options and select the most appropriate action to exploit any situation. All team sports involve players making critical decisions and taking calculated risks in their attempt to create a scoring opportunity. During 15-a-side rugby the decision makers are often only those playing in the influential positions; in seven-a-side every player is continually involved in decision making, and therefore must be repeatedly exposed to conflicting situations in training to gain the necessary experience and expertise.

Because of the considerable amount of space available for the number of players, sevens games are tremendous tactical encounters. Good sevens players are prepared to work patiently, passing the ball around to create an opening in the line of their opponents' defensive formation. Penetrative breakthroughs and scoring opportunities are the result of players applying their skills with guile and subtlety, exploiting the space and developing the advantages that their efforts produce.

As well as a high level of technical efficiency and physical fitness, players must also be confident of their own and their team-mates' abilities. The most successful sevens teams contain players who:

1 are resolute in defence and tenacious tacklers
2 are good ball winners with secure handling skills, capable of resisting the challenges of a tackling player to successfully and accurately distribute possession to a support player when held
3 have good to dynamic acceleration and are balanced, strong and elusive runners
4 are extremely fit and excellent in supporting the player in possession
5 have good anticipation and are able to assess situations quickly and react appropriately
6 are confident and prepared to improvise techniques used to transfer the ball when necessary
7 are consistent performers with a good temperament
8 are part of a well-organised team, and
9 include an accurate and competent goal kicker.

The forwards

Three players normally perform the duties of the forwards, competing in the direct physical contests of the set-piece plays of scrummages, line-outs and kick-offs. Because of the importance of winning possession at every opportunity, care must be taken in selecting a good, balanced unit of players capable of successfully competing, winning, securing and retaining possession of the ball from all the set pieces, as well as during broken play and the transitional phases of ruck and maul.

The players selected to play in the forwards must all be mobile around the field, accomplished in a range of different skills that complement one another to produce a compatible and successful unit. Each member is responsible for performing a certain function at the set-piece plays during the game, all of which are centred around winning and securing possession. When the forwards are unsuccessful in their attempts to win the ball, they must apply their efforts to disrupt and limit the quality of the ball that their opponents secure.

The tight-head prop

This player needs to be the strongest and most powerful of the three forwards, experienced in the art and craft of solid scrummaging. He attempts to dominate and control the opposition at scrummages, helping the hooker to secure good possession.

The hooker

The role of the hooker is a very important and specialist one because the player must be capable of striking quickly to win good, controlled possession at the scrummages and throw the ball accurately into the line-outs.

The loose-head prop

This player performs duties similar to the function of the back-row players in the 15-a-side game, constantly working to secure possession during the transitional phases of play. The loose-head prop also needs to be the specialist line-out jumper, capable of reaching the ball to secure possession at the kick-offs and line-outs.

The threequarters

There are four players in the separate unit of the back division, each capable of creating and exploiting space and converting possession into scoring opportunities. Again it is important to select a balanced unit of players, with each member complementing the strengths and compensating for the limitations and possible minor playing weaknesses of the others.

The performance of every player is obviously important in determining whether or not the team are successful. The achievements of the half-back unit are perhaps the most vital and influential because they are responsible for the team's tactical performance. These decision makers determine the release, direction of movement and the use of the ball, quickly assessing the play and selecting the most appropriate ploys to be executed when in possession. Consequently the threequarters must develop and implement an effective code of signals as a means of communicating their intentions to one another and their team-mates.

The scrum-half

The role of the scrum-half in sevens is exactly the same as in 15-a-side, feeding the ball into the scrummages, exploiting space to make successfu breaks, and transferring the ball to the other threequarters from all phases o play. The scrum-half is very often required to use his passing skills t capitalise on a player securing poor-quality possession, transferring the bal accurately and successfully to the fly-half.

The quality of service to utilise possession and relieve the pressure is th most crucial aspect when distributing the ball from the source of possession This can be accomplished by the application of a wide range of differen techniques, either one- or two-handed, standing or diving, providing th pass is appropriate, effective, accurate and successful in reaching it intended target quickly.

The fly-half

This player controls the tempo of the play when his team are in possession deciding the pace of the game and often the direction of the attack, passin the ball around to create and exploit an opening in the formation of th opposing defensive line. As in 15-a-side, the fly-half is often the decisio maker, with the ability to quickly assess developing situations throughou the ebb and flow of a match.

Because of the responsibilities of the central, pivotal position, the fly-hal needs to have good handling and elusive running skills, with a souno knowledge and understanding of the game, as well as the perceptive abilit to analyse the strengths and weaknesses of all the participating players. Th other members of the team often look to the fly-half to control the game anc for inspiration during play, indicating that this player needs to posses natural leadership qualities to assume the added responsibilities of captaincy.

The centre

He is probably the most direct, committed, physical and aggressive player i the threequarters, capable also of contributing to the elusive cat-and-mous tactics of the team in possession attempting to penetrate the opponents defensive line. The centre continuously applies his skills and talents to creat an attacking opportunity for the nearest support player to exploit.

The winger

This player needs to have the willingness and speed to outsprint and evad the covering defence, to take advantage of the opportunities created by hi team-mates.

The importance of a goal-kicker

The inclusion of a goal-kicker is often a secondary consideration in selectin the players to represent the club in a sevens tournament. Other playing criteria are more significant than the expertise of a specialist goal-kicker. However games can be won and lost by the narrow margin of a missed conversion, and possibly the deciding factor between the selection of two players could be their ability to consistently add the extra points earned from successfully converting the penalty awards and conversions.

The coach

The coach's role is to make sure that every player under his guidance is equipped with the individual skills to help him to participate successfully in rugby football and make a valuable contribution to the performance of his team. The increased space and time available in the seven-a-side game provides players with a more relaxed vehicle for them to demonstrate their skills, expertise, enterprise and commitment. Some players adapt quickly to the demands of seven-a-side rugby and become very capable and successful exponents without ever reaching the same standards of achievement in the 15-a-side game.

During practice sessions the coach is responsible for blending the individuals into a harmonious, cohesive and effective team. Because of the enormous amount of space available during a game, the coach needs to devise suitable defensive and attacking strategies that complement the talents and disguise any limitations of the players. The most important requisite when preparing a team is allocating sufficient time for the players to develop a good understanding, rapport and team spirit.

The structure of training sessions

Players participating in sevens rugby must be physically very fit and therefore capable of recuperating quickly from their exertions during the match. Because the fundamentals of sevens are different from those of the 15-a-side game, coaches are well advised to concentrate a great deal of the available preparation time on players participating in organised seven-a-side practice matches on a full-size playing area.

Participation in controlled seven-a-side games will help players to develop their basic fitness levels as well as the specific fitness and physical conditioning requirements, thereby improving their ability to sustain a continued involvement and contribution to their team's performance. Although the matches are played over seven or ten minutes only, the players are involved in covering great distances at various speeds. The degree of concentration and physical effort required during play can prove exhausting for the players, particularly when both teams are good at retaining possession and the flow of play is continuous, limiting the stoppages and the opportunities to rest and recover.

The training sessions must be well organised and sensibly controlled to prepare the players thoroughly and specifically for sevens rugby. Participation in repetitive unopposed and opposed practices, rehearsing both attacking and defensive strategies from every feature of the game – kick-offs, drop-outs, scrummages, line-outs and penalty moves – will help to establish a suitable and effective pattern of play. However, it is important that the players are encouraged to demonstrate their individual flair and enterprise within the team strategy and game plan. This can be achieved by allowing the play to continue during practice games, liberally applying the advantage rule when possible, to improve the awareness and sharpen the reactions and responses of players.

Restarts

The kick-offs

The reception and execution of the kick-offs are the only certainties that confront a team in playing seven-a-side rugby. Therefore the tactics for these set pieces should be clearly determined, rehearsed and practised regularly to take advantage of the opportunities that exist to secure possession.

The success of a team at starts and restarts can have an important influence on the developments within the game. Winning possession at these set pieces can help to develop confidence among the players and create good attacking positions to exploit.

Receiving the kick-off

At the beginning of the match the team winning the toss of the coin carefully consider the possible effects of the weather conditions and the position of the sun. If no appreciable advantage can be gained and the possible effects are not considered as influential factors in determining which way to play, the captain usually elects to receive the kick-off, intending to begin the game in possession of the ball.

The most important factor when preparing to receive the kick-off is that players are covering as much of the playing area as possible to limit the options available to the opposition. Each player is normally given a predetermined position and the responsibility for covering that particular area of the pitch. However, these positions are flexible and players should react and move to support the player receiving the ball as soon as the intentions of the team kicking off are obvious.

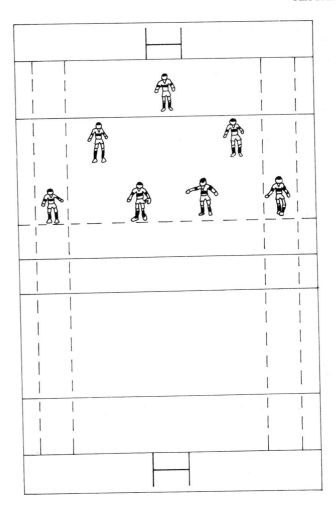

Receiving the kick-off: the 4–2–1 formation

The starting positions for each player can also vary depending on the reason for this particular set piece. At the beginning of games, players assume their predetermined positions but these can change for subsequent receptions of the kick-off. Certain players should be interchangeable and prepared to cover a different start position to save the energy and reduce the work rate of others, without compromising the team's strategic strengths.

The flexibility and movement of players to share the responsibilities should be encouraged, but this tactic should not detract from the overall performance of the seven. For example, when a scoring player has been involved in an extremely long run to the goal line, another player with the appropriate skills can move to cover his start position. It is also important to reduce the workload of the returning goal kicker by possibly changing the

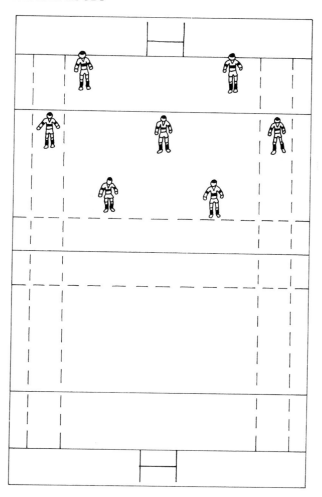

Receiving the kick-off: the 2–3–2 formation

defensive formation to accommodate this player in a position that does not involve running from one end of the pitch to the other.

Because of the tremendous amount of space that players need to cover around the field, there are numerous defensive formations available for the receiving teams. The most important factor to remember is that the object of the receiving players is to secure possession and quickly transfer the ball away from the pressure area, reducing the opportunities for the team kicking off to regain possession. Determining the most suitable and appropriate formation depends on two factors:

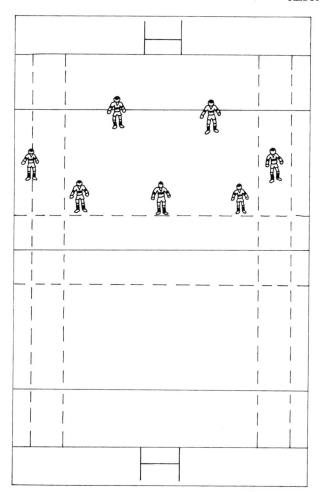

ceiving the kick-off: the 3–2–2 formation

the skills of the players in the seven, and
the intentions of the opposition at the kick-off.

The majority of teams prefer to give themselves an opportunity to regain
ossession from the restart, kicking the ball accurately over the ten-metre
ne and high towards the touchline. This tactic must be countered by the
ceiving team placing their tallest forward, usually the line-out specialist, in
starting position near the touchline to compete for possession. The
ceiving player must quickly assess the flight path of the ball and move to a

position to either catch or make contact with the ball, to guide it back to support player, transferring possession as accurately as possible away from the pressure area.

The other forwards need to be positioned along the ten-metre line to counter the ploy of the other team kicking the ball only the required distance directly along the ground. Keeping the forwards close together at the kick offs is a good tactic because they can function as a unit and use their collective, combative and specialist ball winning skills to secure and retain possession.

Teams rarely use the long, diagonal kick-off in sevens because they have little or no chance of regaining possession, unless they are able to isolate the player receiving the ball. This tactic is possible only when the team fielding the kick-off are deployed inadequately and are much slower players compared to their opponents.

To err on the side of caution in sevens is always the safest policy particularly when receiving the ball from the kick-off when not under pressure. Players can often lose concentration after scoring, or as a result of fatigue, and are always vulnerable to making unnecessary mistakes. The coach must work in realistic game situations, varying the kick-offs to cover numerous options, to improve the concentration levels and attention of the players to avoid any complacency.

When receiving a long kick-off, the waiting player should make sure that possession is secured by using the time available to control and stop the ball with a foot before picking it up. This eliminates any chance of mishandling the ball and prevents the team kicking off from gaining any advantage by exploiting the handling error or quickly retrieving possession at the resulting scrummage. Carefully controlling the ball with the feet when the circumstances allow also gives team-mates more time to move into good support positions.

Providing the team have regularly practised receiving the ball from different and testing kick-offs, players will improve their familiarity with the different situations, be aware of the available options and be able to anticipate developments. Consequently, players will be prepared to alter their positions to nullify the effects of any tactical ploys, variations and strategies implemented by their opponents.

Should the player taking the kick-off overhit the ball, with the result that travels directly into touch, the receiving team should request that the kick off be retaken rather than opt for a scrummage in the centre of the field. Electing to receive the kick-off again increases the pressure on the player starting the game, and improves the chances of securing possession. Opting to restart with a scrummage could prove disadvantageous and improve the prospect of the opposing team securing possession.

Once the team receiving the kick-off have collected and secured possession, all the players should assume good support positions and begin passing the ball around in an attempt to create and exploit an opening in their opponents' defensive line. The narrow or short side of the field always provides numerous opportunities for the team receiving the ball to exploit, particularly when the advancing forwards have committed themselves in competing for possession at the kick-off.

Taking the kick-off

Whether the restart from the half-way line involves a place kick or a drop kick, the most important factor is that the ball is kicked accurately to the intended landing area. The kick-off is the one occasion in sevens when the team in possession are at a disadvantage. This is because their opponents are expecting to receive the ball and have had sufficient time to move into

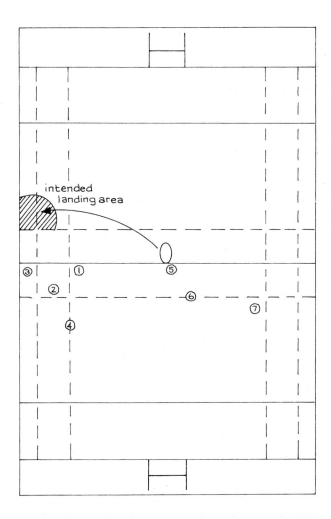

Taking the kick-off: a high, lobbed kick towards the touchline

covering positions and prepare themselves for the delivery of the ball. Obviously this gives the receiving team an advantage and one that the team kicking off must minimise.

Each team should rehearse their intentions at the kick-off to maximise their chances of recovering possession. Kicking the ball into a deep position does not provide a team with any realistic possibility of securing possession quickly, unless they can force the receiving player into a handling error. Therefore the most common tactic is to kick the ball high towards the touchline so that it just crosses the ten-metre line, giving the chasing player a chance to challenge for the ball during its flight.

The chasing player must assess the situation carefully before making a committed challenge to compete for possession from the kick-off, ensuring that there is a very good chance of making contact with the ball. A player should never commit himself unnecessarily, otherwise his efforts are wasted and the team will be exposed and vulnerable until the player recovers his position in the defensive formation. If a player realistically decides that there is little possibility of regaining possession, the team would benefit from the player advancing as part of the defensive line, to prevent the receiving team from immediately exploiting any possible weakness on the narrow side of the field.

It is important that the team kicking off attempt to seize the initiative by disguising their intentions as much as possible. It can be unsettling for a receiving team when they are unable to anticipate and determine the strategy of their opponents from the kick-offs and they must deploy their players around the field to cover numerous options. Hearing the kicking-off team communicating with one another through an agreed code of signals and deliberately pointing out possible gaps in the defensive formation can also cause concern and anxiety among the opposition. Creating doubt and uncertainty in the minds of the players fielding the ball can help to erode their confidence and result in them altering their positions or committing unintentional handling errors.

Preparation is the key to success and players feel more comfortable and confident at the kick-offs when they are able to competently perform a familiar selection of rehearsed strategies. Players should also assess the talents of their opponents and be encouraged to try to exploit any weaknesses that they have observed by concentrating their efforts on particular individuals or an unprotected area of the pitch.

The 22-metre drop-out

This restart does not cause as many problems for the team in possession as the kick-off from the centre of the half-way line because the drop-out can be taken from any point along the 22-metre line. The most successful ploy in retaining possession involves the ball carrier, often the hooker or one of the

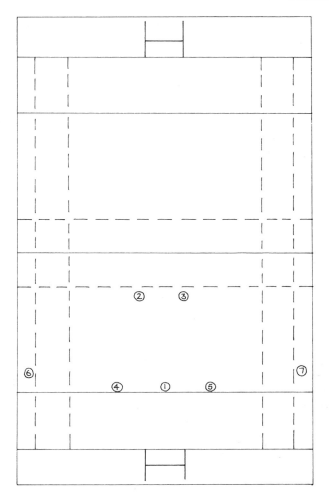

Receiving the 22-metre drop-out

other forwards, creating the space to take a very short drop kick over the 22-metre line, and in one movement driving forwards to collect the ball and immediately passing it directly backwards between the legs to a supporting player.

There are occasions when a team uses the opportunity to kick the ball deep into their opponents' half in an attempt to exploit poor field positioning, creating a kick-and-chase or line-out situation. Attempting to relieve pressure by kicking the ball deep must be very carefully considered because of the great risk of losing possession. Drop-kicking the ball into space behind the opposing team can prove effective in sevens when either the chasing players are much quicker than their opponents, or the ball is deliberately kicked to bounce into touch to improve the field position, restarting the game with a line-out further upfield. Because possession is vitally important in sevens it should not be wasted or given away unnecessarily.

Successfully defending against the 22-metre drop-out is difficult because the team in possession have a distinct advantage and are able to control the proceedings. All the defending players must react quickly and move into positions that limit the space available and hopefully delay the efforts of the team in possession to create an immediate attacking opportunity from this restart.

The set pieces

There are numerous attacking opportunities from every set piece that occurs during sevens, because the three forwards and the scrum-half from each team are committed to these restarts in a concentrated area. The remainder of the field is available for the threequarters to exploit when they have possession.

Winning possession from set pieces obviously has tremendous significance and is vitally important in determining the outcome of many games. Therefore the forwards and scrum-half need to work very hard to develop a good rapport and understanding, with successful strategies to implement as a unit to win their own ball. When one team have the advantage of the feed to the set pieces, the opposing forwards should attempt to disrupt their efforts to minimise the benefits from winning good, quick possession.

Scrummages

There are normally more scrummages than line-outs during sevens games, which increases the value and importance of this set piece. The forwards and the scrum-half need to practise scrummaging until they can guarantee securing possession. Every player involved has an important role to play: the props need to support the hooker in a comfortable and advantageous start position to allow for a quick and successful strike for the ball; the scrum-half and the hooker need to perfect their communications to ensure that the delivery of the ball into the scrummage occurs immediately when the hooker signals.

The success of the performance of the forwards and the scrum-half are totally dependent on one another. The code of signals that they devise should help to synchronise their actions, with the props driving their opponents backwards when the ball is put into the scrummage, helping the hooker to strike quickly and win possession.

The speed and control of the strike by the hooker will determine the quality of the possession, because there are no other forwards to channel the ball for the scrum-half. However, there are two possible options available for the hooker to directly guide the ball for the scrum-half to collect: channel one is through the legs of the loose-head prop, and channel two is through the space between the non-striking foot of the hooker and the inside foot of the loose-head prop.

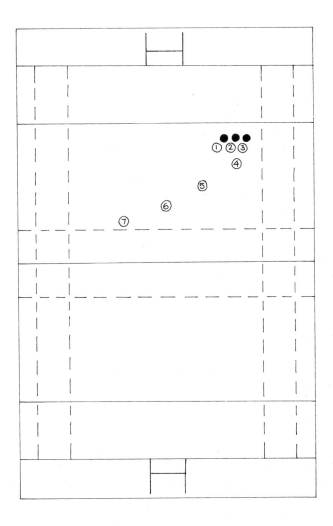

An attacking threequarters alignment at the scrummage

There are advantages and disadvantages involved in directing the ball through either channel. It must be the collective decision of the forwards and the scrum-half to determine the more suitable, satisfactory and successful for them. Channel one produces quicker ball compared with the slightly improved protection that Channel two provides the scrum-half with. The factor determining the decision concerns the ability of the players involved in the scrummages to win, secure and utilise possession.

The team putting the ball into the scrummages have a definite advantage. However, the opposing unit of forwards must be prepared to nullify the

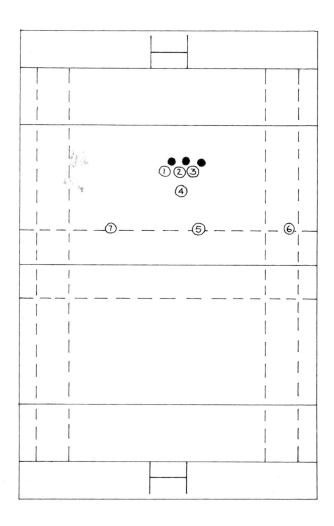

The threequarters are positioned to support the half-backs should they direct an attack to either side of the scrummage

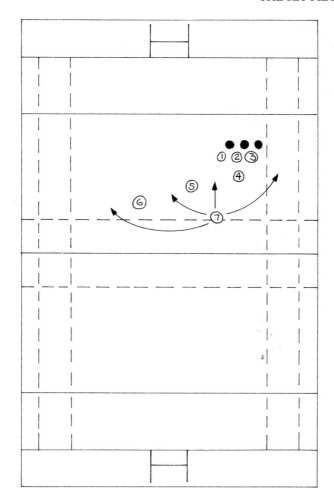

The winger can enter the threequarter line in numerous positions, hopefully to penetrate the opposition's defensive formation

advantage by attempting to disrupt the scrummages, making it as difficult as possible to win good-quality possession. The main intention of the forwards and the scrum-half should be to deny their opponents any opportunities to exploit and develop their advantage of putting the ball into the scrummage.

There are four different tactical ploys that can be implemented to overturn and spoil the advantage:

1 the synchronised effort of all three forwards driving their opponents backwards and off the ball

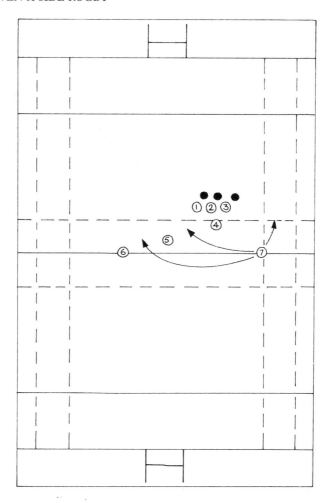

The winger, positioned on the narrow side of the field, must be prepared to support the attack in numerous places in the threequarter line

2 the hooker and/or tight-head prop striking to win the ball against the head
3 the hooker kicking the ball through the gap in the legs of the other players for the scrum-half to chase, pressurise and hopefully secure possession, or
4 wheeling the scrummage.

It is important that the signals of communication between the forwards and the scrum-half are impossible for the opposition to decipher. It is possible for a team to counter every tactical ploy when they are forewarned,

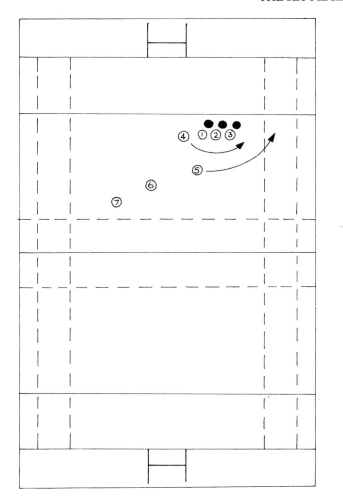

The half-backs exploiting the space on the narrow side of the field

allowing them to benefit from their opponents' intended endeavours. Every attempt to disrupt the other team's efforts contains an element of risk, but the possibility of securing unexpected possession could prove decisive during sevens.

Once the outcome of the scrummage is determined, every player must be aware of his immediate responsibilities. The unit winning the ball must continue driving forwards to commit their opponents and delay them breaking from the set piece. The forwards losing possession need to release themselves from their binding as quickly as possible, to move into position in

Good covering positions by defending half-backs at the scrummage, with players capable of moving in either direction

their team's defensive formation. The scrum-half of the team losing possession should also move backwards to defend against any attacks close to the scrummage.

Line-outs

Teams are able to achieve tremendous attacking opportunities from the line-out because the laws of the game require the threequarters to stand ten metres away from the forwards involved in this set piece. Once again the team responsible for the throw-in have a distinct advantage over their opponents. During practice sessions the players can devise an extensive repertoire of numerous tactical ploys and variations to exploit the advantage of the throw-in.

The most important factor determining the range of possible tactical ploys and variations is the ability of the thrower to deliver the ball accurately into the line-out. The hooker is the most likely player to be given the responsibility for taking the throw-in, but only if this player is reliable and successful at performing the task. The throw-in is so important that the formation of the team can be altered if necessary to ensure that the most consistently accurate player is used, regardless of position.

Innovative thinking to develop strategies that accommodate and involve different players in throwing the ball into the line-out can possibly improve the success rate of winning possession at these contests. A team may be able to initiate better attacking opportunities by altering the positions of players and utilising their particular strengths in unusual situations. For example:

1 substituting the positions and roles of the winger and hooker at the line-outs can cause confusion and uneasiness among the opposition, creating a situation in which two players with conflicting skills and different abilities are in direct competition with one another

2 using the scrum-half to take the throw-ins, before moving behind the players in the line-out to perform the more typical duties, can release the hooker to move among the threequarters and create an overlap situation.

It is important that the players are confident and achieve greater success than otherwise in applying these positional changes effectively. The team's overall performance should improve and not compromise any players or create any unnecessary difficulties. Introducing positional changes can help a team to seize the initiative because they can unnerve their opponents and break their concentration.

Teams should rehearse and develop an extensive repertoire of ploys that they can perform consistently and successfully at the line-out, to help them to secure possession and prevent their opponents from achieving the same. There are numerous options available to all the players involved in this set piece and, as always, it is often the simplest that proves the most effective.

The following are a selection of tactical ploys that can be rehearsed and perfected in training. All involve an accurate throw-in.

a The ball is quickly thrown into the line-out before the opposing players have had time to prepare to receive the ball.

b The ball is thrown to a player deliberately arriving late and exploiting any available space at the front or back of the line-out.

c The throw is timed and delivered to the first or second player to catch or deflect the ball to the scrum-half.

d The two forwards move away from the five-metre line and increase the distance between one another, creating gaps at the front of the line-out and between themselves to be exploited by one of the forwards moving into the space to receive the ball, or the scrum-half moving into the space to catch the ball and driving into or past the opposing half-back.

e The two forwards move around to distract their opponents, making it difficult for them to determine the distance or anticipate the intended receiver of the throw-in.

f The ball is thrown over the top of the line-out for the scrum-half or one of the threequarters to receive. This ploy can be particularly effective when the line-out is less than ten metres from the goal line of the team with the responsibility of the throw-in and they can take advantage of the fact that their threequarters are closer to the line-out than their opponents. Providing one of the threequarters is capable of catching or collecting the ball while running, this tactic provides a good attacking opportunity.

g The ball is thrown low to allow the front player at the line-out to kick the ball forwards along the touchline for the others to chase and pressurise the other team. This ploy can be successful when the team are using the winger to take the throw-in or have much quicker players than their opponents.

The variety and extent of the repertoire of attacking ploys will be limited by

1 the skill level and competence of the players involved
2 the playing conditions, which can affect the performance of both teams and limit the number of ploys that can be successfully implemented during games played in inclement weather. It is difficult for the player with the responsibility for the throw-in to execute an accurate and controlled delivery in high winds or with a slippery ball.

Developing an unbreakable code of signals for the players to communicate their intentions to one another is vitally important to co-ordinate the efforts of all the players involved in the line-outs. Good communication between the players is necessary to prepare them for their particular roles and synchronise the timing of the throw-in with the actions of the target player attempting to win possession.

Rucks and mauls

Once the ball has been won and transferred away from the set pieces, the players are responsible for retaining possession for as long as possible, to frustrate their opponents from creating any attacking or scoring opportunities. The defending players must work hard to pressurise the attacking team, trying to force them into performing handling errors or succeeding in tackling a player in possession.

If the ball carrier is held in the tackle, it should be possible to transfer possession to a support player. Problems of retaining possession should only occur when the ball carrier is grounded in the tackle, or has the movement of both arms restricted and is not capable of passing the ball to another player.

When tackled in possession, the ball carrier should attempt to stay upright, allowing him to assess the developments of the game, attempting to accurately distribute the ball to a team mate, or successfully creating a target for the nearest support players to develop a maul. Holding the ball in an accessible position helps players to secure and retain possession, successfully limiting the efforts of the opposition attempting to recover and smuggle the ball. It is important that every player in the seven is capable of mauling, because at every breakdown in the continuity of play, when the ball carrier is tackled in possession, the nearest player should help to secure and retain possession.

Rucking is a rare occurrence in sevens because it is much more successful to pass the ball backwards towards a support player than to risk going to ground in possession and releasing the ball to create an open contest between the nearest players from either team. When the ball carrier is forced to the ground in the tackle and required to release the ball, the nearest support player should quickly pick it up to secure possession and pass it away from the pressure area. Rucking does not secure possession because the ball remains on the ground and available for the next player to arrive at the breakdown, and that could equally be an opponent, rather than a colleague.

Players should be committed to securing the ball when a breakdown occurs, but must be cautious about involving themselves in contesting for possession and careful that they do not neglect their other defensive duties. Two players should be able to compete for the ball in the transitional phases of the mauls, releasing the other players to cover and hold their defensive line. If more players commit themselves to the breakdown, their team could be short of defensive cover to prevent the quick break should their opponents win the ball.

There are occasions when players will decide to participate in the breakdown to ensure that their team do secure possession or prevent the other team from dominating the proceedings. Should more than two players from one team commit themselves to the breakdown – and there are occasions when this will happen, either intentionally or unnecessarily – those players must succeed in their efforts to secure possession, otherwise their team-mates will be exposed and extremely vulnerable.

Once the ball is moved away from the breakdown, every player must quickly recover his position and continue to fulfil his responsibilities, either supporting the attack or covering in defence. The team that are able to regroup their players quickly could prove the more successful in exploiting an attacking opportunity or managing to frustrate their opponents' efforts.

After the flow and continuity of the game is broken, sound defensive play requires tremendous organisation and good discipline. The recovering players must immediately assess the developing situations and move into positions to help to counter the actions of their opponents. Every player must be aware of his individual roles in the team formation and understand his responsibilities within the defensive strategy.

Defensive strategies and formations

Defending in seven-a-side involves players exerting as much pressure as possible on the team in possession, attempting to restrict the number of options by limiting the amount of space and time available. Players must work hard to maintain their defensive formation to cover across the field, attempting to minimise any forward progress and force an opponent to commit a handling error to restrict his achievements.

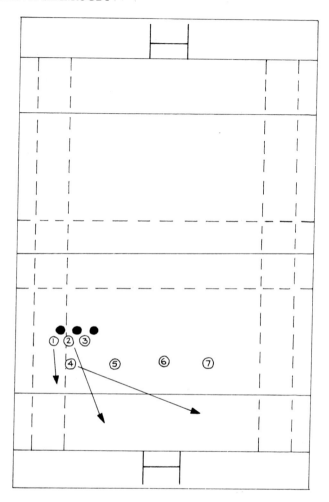

Defensive formation and support positions to reinforce the cover across the field

To exert continual pressure on the team in possession, the defending players usually stand in a line across the field. Each player is responsible for the area or zone immediately surrounding his position and must prevent any opponent from breaching the defensive blanket at any point in that channel. Because of the continual movement of the ball and incidents that occur during play, the areas of individual responsibility constantly change. However, the basic principle of the blanket coverage of defenders spread in one line across the field always applies, requiring players to move quickly in support of one another during the flow of the game.

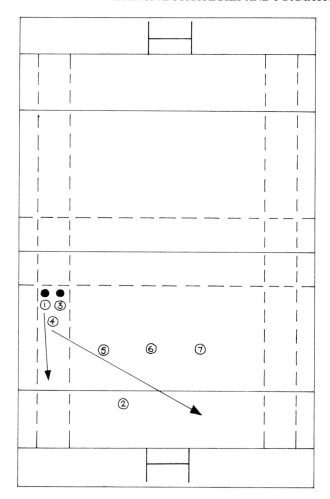

efensive strategy following a line-out, highlighting the support positions to reinforce the ⟶ver across the field

There are variations that have developed from this basic formation, with ⟩me teams preferring to remove one player from the defensive line to cover ⟨ehind the front players. This player performs a similar role to the full-back ⟩ 15-a-side, following the ball across the field to cover any breaks or kicks ⟩head. A second tactical development involves one player assuming a more ⟩rward position than the others and continually chasing the ball across the ⟨ld, directly pressurising the receiving player.

Choosing the most suitable defensive strategy again depends on the ⟨bilities and talents of the players selected. The blanket coverage of the field

– with the seven players in a line across it – and the sweeper system are th
most popular defensive formations. Both strategies have obvious advantage
and disadvantages; the selection and use of one or the other should be base
on the collective playing strengths of the team's seven members. Because th
requirements of the chasing player's role are so demanding, this strategy ca
only be implemented successfully for a short period of time, should the nee
arise to exert greater pressure on the team with the ball.

The use of possession

The importance of winning and securing possession has been covered i
previous sections; retention and strategic and effective use of the ball are th
relevant factors that determine the performance and affect the eventua
outcome of the game. Because of the size of the playing area and the reduce
number of participants, players have numerous opportunities to displa
their individual handling abilities and elusive-running skills.

The key to success involves players identifying the most appropriate
situation and opportune moment to perform a particular skill to take
advantage of any weaknesses in their opponents' defensive formation. The
ball carrier must always maintain contact with the other players and resis
any temptation to run into an isolated area in an attempt to breach the
defending cover. Retention of the ball is vital and should always be the prio
consideration when assessing and calculating the risks involved in executing
a particular attacking ploy.

The ball carrier must make a quick assessment of the playing situation and
decide which action would be the most effective and appropriate. Individual
moments of inspiration and enterprise can win matches but, for the majority
of the game, players must work together, supporting one another and
running off the ball. Good anticipation and close support play can turn a
half break into a scoring opportunity and help a team to retain possession
should the ball carrier be tackled.

Players running off the ball can also create numerous options for the
player in possession to deceive the defenders, using the support player as a
decoy. Practising numerous passing movements and ploys during training
should help to build an extensive and effective repertoire of attacking
stratagems. All the passing ploys demonstrated in 15-a-side can prove even
more devastating in sevens, particularly the dummy pass and switch, dummy
switch, loop and miss moves.

Once the space has been created, the ball carrier must accelerate through
the gap to develop and exploit the attacking opportunity. It is the
responsibility of the other players to move quickly and support the ball
carrier, to gain the maximum possible advantage from the break. However

the actions of the player in possession can sometimes surprise his team-mates, and the circumstances can prevent or delay the arrival of close support. Under these circumstances, when it is not possible to score, it could prove more beneficial for the ball carrier to slow down or return back towards the support to eliminate the risk of being tackled when isolated and consequently lose possession.

Kicking during open play

A player must have a very good reason to kick the ball ahead when his team are in possession. There are many options available to a player because of the amount of space on the pitch, but the selection of the most appropriate and successful action is determined by the player's intention and motives. Accurate kicking into space to create a scoring opportunity or relieve pressure can be a very effective tactic in sevens. A team electing to kick the ball during open play can benefit providing they are able to quickly recover possession further upfield and gain a definite territorial advantage and considerably improve their field position.

Success often revolves around players executing the unexpected and inspirational: kicking the ball ahead can sometimes prove beneficial and should be carefully considered as a possible tactic in certain circumstances. There are many possible situations in which a team can benefit from kicking the ball, ranging from the long diagonal kick – to waste time and pressurise the opposition – to the short, chip kick – used to breach a fast-approaching, flat line of defenders.

Penalty moves

Each team can benefit considerably from developing a repertoire of penalty moves that they have rehearsed and are able to perform successfully. Every player must be aware of his role in the proceedings as soon as the captain communicates the signal announcing the selection of a particular penalty ploy. Therefore to avoid confusion the devised code of signals should be easily communicated and simple to interpret and understand.

Attacking at penalty moves

Although it could prove advantageous to devise elaborate and intricate penalty moves, the time spent on explaining individual roles and perfecting their execution could be better used on other aspects of seven-a-side rugby. Often the simple and straightforward penalty moves are the most successful because they are difficult to defend against.

An obvious example is the quickly taken, short, tapped penalty kick that does not allow the opposition to realign or recover their defensive formation. When the referee awards a penalty, the player nearest the ball should immediately secure possession and decide whether or not to seize the opportunity to quickly play the ball and exploit the poor positioning and coverage of the defenders. Delaying the execution of the short, tapped penalty kick reduces its effectiveness because the defending team are able to reorganise and deploy their players in good defensive positions.

There are various other options available for the attacking team, including kicking for touch to improve territorial position, or taking a place or drop kick at goal when in range. However, these ploys lack enterprise and possibly sacrifice valuable possession if the execution of the kick is poor or the attempt to score is unsuccessful. To run the ball at penalties can prove much more rewarding, and a score requires the opposition to restart the game by kicking the ball back to the attacking team, allowing them to monopolise possession.

The team awarded the penalty have a definite advantage because they are guaranteed possession, and the defending players are required by the laws of the game to retreat ten metres from the mark of the penalty. Each situation always provides a different set of circumstances, but the team awarded the penalty should attempt to exploit the opportunities that exist by handling the ball. Executing a varied repertoire of well-rehearsed penalty moves, disguising intentions, the direction of movement and point of the attack, makes it even more difficult for the defending team to successfully counter.

Occasionally a defending player can succeed in deliberately delaying the attacking team taking a quick, short, tapped penalty kick, allowing team-mates to recover their position in the defensive formation. When the team awarded the penalty are prevented from sustaining the continuity and flow of the game to exploit any numerical advantage, they must review the situation and consider the different options available.

It is usual that each player assumes the same start position for each penalty move, otherwise the intentions of the ploy may become obvious to the opponents. However, the starting positions can be intentionally varied in one or two ploys to deliberately attract the attention of the defending team. Creating an element of doubt and uncertainty in the defenders' minds can prove beneficial. Moving a particular player into an unusual starting position can cause the defending team to alter their formation to counter the change. If a defender does not move to cover the possibility of the player receiving the ball, then the attacking team must exploit the opportunity.

The scrum-half will normally be responsible for taking the organised short, tapped penalty kick to restart the game, once the other players are in position to execute a rehearsed ploy. Below are several ploys that a team can

ractise to perfect and extend their repertoire of moves to take advantage of
ne penalty award.

loy 1 The scrum-half runs directly across the field and offers the ball to
ach of the threequarters running straight, executing a scissors or dummy
cissors move with the player who can benefit most from receiving
ossession.

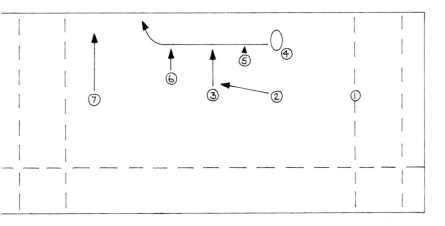

*he scrum-half moves across the field, executing a passing move with the most suitable
hreequarter*

loy 2 The scrum-half links with the fly-half before looping around to
eceive a return pass, then executes a scissors with the centre or winger.

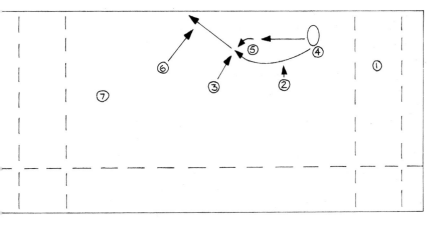

he scrum-half executing a passing move with the fly-half and then the centre or winger

Ploy 3 The scrum-half loops both the fly-half and centre in turn, before linking up with the winger and forwards running in support.

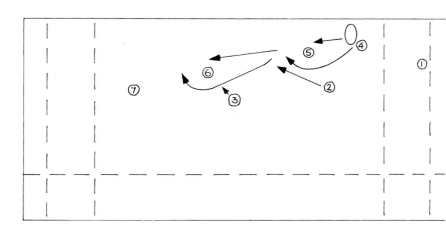

The scrum-half loops the fly-half and centre

Ploy 4 The fly-half dummies the pass to the looping scrum-half, transferring the ball to one of the forwards running across to the open side, linking up with the majority of the other players.

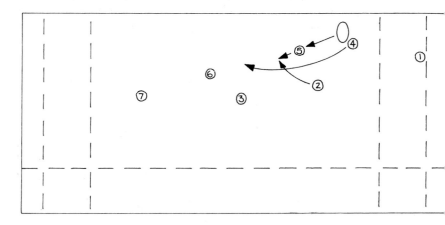

Using a dummy pass to alter the angle of attack and improve the number of support players outside the ball-carrier

Ploy 5 Again, the run of the looping scrum-half is a decoy and the fly-half passes the ball to one of the forwards running across to the narrow side.

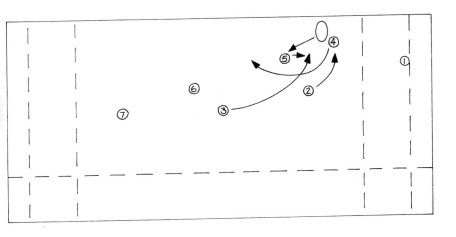

The scrum-half is used as a decoy again

Ploy 6 When the penalty is awarded close to the opponents' goal line, the attacking players move further away than usual from the scrum-half and begin running quickly towards the ball when given the agreed signal. The scrum-half allows the players almost to reach the point of the penalty before kicking the ball through the mark and passing to one of the advancing players. The momentum and strength should enable the player receiving the ball to drive beyond the efforts of the defenders to score.

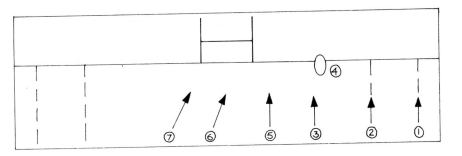

Taking a penalty close to the opponents' goal line

Defending at penalty moves

The defending players need to legitimately delay their opponents taking the awarded penalty and restrict the number of attacking opportunities by quickly recovering their defensive formation of blanket coverage across the field to limit the space available. Each player in the defending team has responsibility for a designated channel of the field and must also react to the actions of his opposite number and assume a corresponding position.

Sound defence requires good organisation, anticipation, awareness of developments and speed of action to counter the movements of the other team. When the ball is positioned on the mark denoted by the referee, the defending team must designate one player to watch and cover the player nearest the ball and communicate when the penalty kick has been taken. This is a worthwhile deployment, because the movement of the opposing players could be a ploy to distract the attention of the defenders away from the ball.

When the penalty is taken, the defenders must advance in the blanket formation to limit the amount of space available for the attacking players to complete the individual assignments of their ploy. If the penalty ploy is an intricate movement, the advance of the defensive blanket of players can reduce its effectiveness or possibly result in tackling a player in possession of the ball. When an attacking team are executing a penalty move with a pivot player, extra pressure can be applied by designating one defending player to sprint towards the pivot, attempting to tackle the player in possession and prevent the completion of the planned move.

If one player is used to attack and pressurise the pivot, the rest of the team are responsibile for covering a larger area of the field. Therefore the chasing player must be capable of redirecting his efforts should the ball be transferred quickly by the pivot, and resume his position covering a zone to contribute to the defensive formation of his team. Once the ball is played and passed along the line of attacking players, the defenders should move forwards and across as a unit, to shepherd and shadow the movement of the ball, putting as much pressure as possible on their opponents.

Because the defensive formation consists only of a line of players spread across the field, there is little or no cover, even if the team use a sweeper system. Therefore aggressive and decisive tackling is vitally important during all phases of play. Should a player breach the defence, it is difficult for the defenders to recover unless the attacking player lacks pace. The team must maintain their defensive alignment, and solid, tenacious tackling prevents a player from penetrating their formation.